WALKING – – – – –→
MILWAUKEE

WALKING ----->
MILWAUKEE

31 Tours of Brew City's Neighborhoods, Landmarks, and Entertainment Districts

First Edition

Royal Brevväxling and Molly Snyder

 WILDERNESS PRESS ... *on the trail since 1967*

Walking Milwaukee: 31 Tours of Brew City's Neighborhoods, Landmarks, and Entertainment Districts
First edition, third printing 2024
Copyright © 2020 by Royal Brevväxling and Molly Snyder

Project editor: Kate Johnson
Maps: Scott McGrew
Cover and interior design: Jonathan Norberg
Interior photos by Royal Brevväxling and Molly Snyder, except page 157 (Walt M/Shutterstock)
Proofreader: Emily Beaumont
Indexer: Frances Lennie

Library of Congress Cataloging-in-Publication Data

Names: Brevväxling, Royal, 1970– author. | Snyder, Molly, 1970– author.
Title: Walking Milwaukee : 31 tours of Brew City's neighborhoods, landmarks, and entertain-
    ment districts / Royal Brevväxling and Molly Snyder.
Description: First edition. | Birmingham, AL : Wilderness Press, 2020. | Includes bibliographical
    references and index.
Identifiers: LCCN 2020016533 (print) | LCCN 2020016534 (ebook) | ISBN 9781643590202 (pbk.)
    | ISBN 9781643590219 (ebook)
Subjects: LCSH: Milwaukee (Wis.)—Tours. | Milwaukee (Wis.)—Guidebooks. | Walking—
    Wisconsin—Milwaukee—Guidebooks.
Classification: LCC F589.M63 B74 2020 (print) | LCC F589.M63 (ebook) | DDC 977.5/95—dc23
LC record available at https://lccn.loc.gov/2020016533
LC ebook record available at https://lccn.loc.gov/2020016534

Published by  **WILDERNESS PRESS**
    An imprint of AdventureKEEN
    2204 First Ave. S., Ste. 102
    Birmingham, AL 35233
    800-678-7006, fax 877-374-9016

Visit wildernesspress.com for a complete listing of our books and for ordering information. Contact us
at our website, at facebook.com/wildernesspress1967, or at twitter.com/wilderness1967 with questions
or comments. To find out more about who we are and what we're doing, visit blog.wildernesspress.com.

Manufactured in China
Distributed by Publishers Group West

Frontispiece: Captain Pabst Pilot House (see Walk 2, page 8)
Cover photo: Milwaukee skyline at twilight by f11photo/Shutterstock

SAFETY NOTICE: Although Wilderness Press and the authors have made every attempt to ensure that
the information in this book is accurate at press time, they are not responsible for any loss, damage, injury,
or inconvenience that may occur to anyone while using this book. You are responsible for your own
safety and health while following the walking trips described here. Always check local conditions, know
your limitations, and consult a map.

As this book went to press in 2020, the coronavirus pandemic was threatening the future of many
local businesses. If you plan to visit businesses along the walking routes in this book, consider calling
ahead of time or checking their websites.

Authors' Note and Dedication

We started writing this book in the fall of 2018, long before we had ever heard the word *coronavirus*. We imagined this book coming out during a lively and exciting time for Milwaukee, when the city was bursting with festivals and events (including a very large national convention). Instead, we completed this guide knowing that it would be received by a different audience, one turned more inward than out. We now hope our words and photos encourage people to get out and explore our resilient city in new and safer ways. Milwaukeeans have so much to offer, regardless of hardships, and so this book is heartfully dedicated to them.

Table of Contents

Walking Milwaukee

Introduction

Milwaukee is a small town/big city amalgam with a world-class arena and art museum that are within walking distance from mom-and-pop taverns and eateries.

The city is perched on the shore of beautiful, always-changing-in-color Lake Michigan, so water is integral to the Milwaukee experience. It's the lifeblood of beer, the tradition of Friday night fish fries, and a constant reminder of the vast unknown that has contributed to the city's progressive politics in the past.

Since the mid-1800s, Milwaukee has been a big fish in the brewing industry, and today Molson Coors (formerly MillerCoors) produces 8.5 million barrels of beer every year. In recent years, Milwaukee has also bred many microbreweries that continue to manifest the "Brew City" moniker. Thus, going on a brewery tour in Milwaukee is practically mandatory.

Milwaukee embraces its wholesome, hardworking *Happy Days* past—the popular 1970s–'80s sitcom was based in Wisconsin's largest city—and will forever be the home of Harley-Davidson motorcycles (the first Harley was invented here in 1903). At the same time, it also strives to shed its shadow sides that include segregation and a famous serial killer.

What results is a city that respects the past while it moves boldly and kindly into the future. Slowly but surely, it's creating opportunities for natives and guests alike, thanks to recent amenities such as the streetcar, called The Hop, along with the influx of contemporary entertainment spots and options.

Like most places worth visiting—and like the Great Lake it lives next to—Milwaukee has a flow of its own, one that's definitely worth sailing.

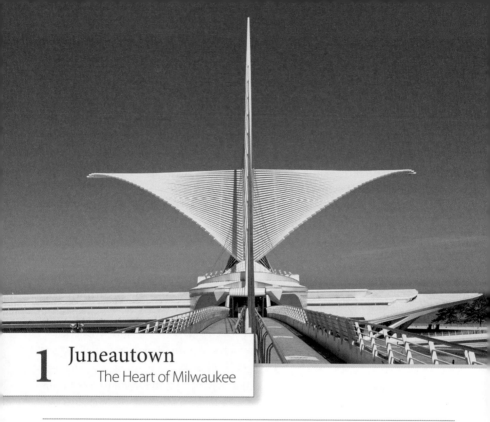

1 Juneautown
The Heart of Milwaukee

BOUNDARIES: N. Water St., E. Juneau Ave., N. Prospect Ave., E. Wisconsin Ave.
DISTANCE: 3 miles
DIFFICULTY: Easy
PARKING: Public parking is available in the structure beneath O'Donnell Park, across the street from the Milwaukee Art Museum
PUBLIC TRANSIT: MCTS routes 33 and Gold

Milwaukee, the largest city in Wisconsin, lies on Lake Michigan at the confluence of the Milwaukee, Menomonee, and Kinnickinnic Rivers. The downtown area employs the largest number of people in the state, serves as a cultural and artistic hub, and hosts national sporting events.

Currently referred to as East Town, downtown Milwaukee between the river and the lake was formerly known as Juneautown, and the west side of the river as Kilbourntown, after settlers Solomon Juneau and Byron Kilbourn, respectively. Kilbourn's rivalry with the settlement on the east side of the river caused Milwaukee's 1845 Bridge War and the creation of today's still-disjointed street patterns from one side of the river to the other.

Juneau, a Frenchman born in 1793 near Montreal, Canada, arrived in the area in the employ of Jacques Vieau's fur-trading company. Juneau married his boss's daughter, Josette, and the couple stuck around, helping to cofound what would later become the city of Milwaukee.

Upon Juneau's arrival, today's East Town was already home to the Potawatomi, Menominee, and Ho-Chunk, among other First Nations peoples who used the Milwaukee River and its many tributaries stretching 100 miles to the north. Juneau's Native American trading partners gave the merchant, real estate developer, and future mayor the nickname Solomo.

Walk Description

Starting at the exit from the parking structure beneath O'Donnell Park, cross Lincoln Memorial Drive at the stoplight to the ❶ **Milwaukee Art Museum.** Founded in 1888, the museum is home to more than 31,000 works of art, including pieces by Wisconsin native Georgia O'Keeffe. Along with renowned collections of American folk and decorative arts, German Expressionist prints, and German and Austrian paintings, the Richard and Erna Flagg Collection of Haitian Art is also particularly wonderful. In 2001, Spanish architect Santiago Calatrava created the Quadracci Pavilion with the astounding, movable brise-soleil that when open has a 217-foot "wingspan." The structure remains closed at night and during harsh weather. The expanded white wings have become an unofficial logo for Milwaukee in recent years.

Take the stairs in front of the museum to walk across the pedestrian bridge and step onto the plaza with ❷ *The Calling,* an orange starburst-looking sculpture, straight ahead. This is O'Donnell Park (it's on top of the parking structure).

Constructed from steel beams, *The Calling* was made by American artist Mark di Suervo and erected in 1981. Milwaukeeans are divided in their feelings toward the structure, some finding it simple and cheerful, others describing it as ugly, dated, and blocking views of the museum's winglike structure. From a distance up Wisconsin Avenue, The Calling appears to stand in the exact middle of the art museum's beloved addition. In its defense, Calatrava is said to have incorporated The Calling when designing and placing his addition to the museum.

Head west (straight ahead) on Wisconsin Avenue. On the left, the ❸ **Betty Brinn Children's Museum** is a not-for-profit, hands-on museum that opened in 1995 and appeals primarily to kids ages 1–10. It is named for Betty Brinn, a Milwaukee native who grew up in 15 foster homes and later worked to help low-income women and kids receive medical care and insurance.

Continue west on Wisconsin Avenue, noting on the left the U.S. Bank Center Building, which is the tallest in Milwaukee. Northwestern Mutual, a Fortune 500 financial services organization, occupies the structures on the right, both old and tall-modern-shimmering-glass new. The Milwaukee Federal Building and US courthouse is ahead on the left, and on your right is the ❹ **Wisconsin Gas Building** with the massive "flame" on its roof. The Art Deco Gas Light Building (as it's sometimes called) was built in 1930 and designed by Milwaukee architect Alexander Eschweiler. It features different materials on its facade that blend from dark to light, but the structure's most stunning feature is a 21-foot, 4-ton weather beacon shaped like a natural-gas flame that indicates the weather forecast by its color and flicker. Many Milwaukeeans know this rhyme to remember what the flame colors mean in terms of forecast:

When the flame is red, it's warm weather ahead.
When the flame is gold, watch out for cold.
When the flame is blue, there's no change in view.
When there's a flickering flame, expect snow or rain.

Two blocks ahead on the right is ❺ **The Pfister,** Milwaukee's most notable hotel. It was built in 1893 based on a vision shared by businessman Guido Pfister and his son, Charles. The goal was to create "Milwaukee's living room." Over the decades, the lavish hotel survived bankruptcies and decay. Today it is owned by the Marcus Corporation and welcomes guests, celebrities, and athletes from around the world. It is also home to Blu, a cocktail lounge on the 23rd floor with one of the best views of the city, as well as the cozy Lobby Lounge and a casual café on the ground floor.

The intersection of East Wisconsin Avenue and North Water Street has been a hub of retail and commercial industry since before Solomon Juneau opened up shop on its northwest corner. ❻ **The Iron Block,** on the intersection's southeast corner, is an ornate building made with state-of-the-art 1860 technology, such as fireproofing.

Turn right (north) on Water Street. It was also near here that Juneau founded Wisconsin's oldest newspaper, the *Milwaukee Sentinel,* in 1837, which merged with its rival in 1995 to form the *Milwaukee Journal Sentinel.* Along this stretch, check out the historic 16-story ❼ **City Center at 735** office building on the left. Designed by architect Daniel Burnham, the building opened in 1914 as First Wisconsin National Bank. Current tenants include ❽ *OnMilwaukee,* a digital media company and online daily magazine and city guide founded in 1998.

Take a left on East Mason Street, go a quarter block toward the Riverwalk, and take a right in the alley, also known as Front Street. The original ❾ **SafeHouse** is an iconic James Bond–themed bar and restaurant that's a challenge to find and then a challenge to actually get into because it requires a specific password that hasn't changed since the bar opened in 1966. But don't worry, the door person is there to help by encouraging shenanigans in exchange for entrance. A second SafeHouse opened in Chicago in 2017.

Take a right on East Wells Street. On the left at the intersection with Water Street is the landmark ⑩ **Pabst Theater,** built in 1895. Named after beer brewer Frederick Pabst, who footed the bill for its construction, the building remained in his family until the mid-20th century and is now operated as part of the Pabst Theater Group, which also includes the Riverside and the ballroom inside Turner Hall, among other venues.

Turn left (north) on North Water Street. On the right, ⑪ **Milwaukee City Hall** is a Flemish Renaissance Revival–style building designed by prominent Milwaukee architect Henry C. Koch and built in 1895. Its 11-ton bell is named Solomon Juneau, after the Milwaukee cofounder and first mayor.

In the next two blocks on the left are ⑫ **Saint Kate,** Milwaukee's arts hotel that opened in 2019, and the ⑬ **Marcus Performing Arts Center,** which hosts the Milwaukee Symphony Orchestra (until fall/winter 2020), the Florentine Opera, First Stage Children's Theater, and many big-name touring shows.

In the middle of a stretch of popular Water Street bars, take a right on East Juneau Avenue. What remains of the early industrial powerhouse Blatz Brewing Company is visible in the form of an office and residential complex. ⑭ **Milwaukee School of Engineering (MSOE),** a private university offering bachelor's and master's degrees primarily in engineering, stretches across many buildings to the north and south. It is also home to independent/college radio station WMSE 91.7.

In 0.3 mile take a right on North Jackson Street. ⑮ **Cathedral Square Park** is located on the right—across from Cathedral of Saint John the Evangelist. The public green space hosts a farmers

Milwaukee City Hall

market, Bastille Days French Festival, Jazz in the Park every Thursday night in the summertime, and holiday events centered around the park's massive Christmas decorations.

Take a right on East Wells Street, walking along the south end of the park. Anchored in the middle of the next block is LGBTQ cocktail lounge and venue **⑯ This Is It,** the oldest still-operating gay bar in Milwaukee, opened in 1968. As cultural attitudes have changed, the bar has slowly developed a more prominent street facade. Customers formerly entered from the alley, and the front door was there only as required by law. Recently This Is It acquired part of the space next door for room to create a dance area and add a second bar, and the city painted the nearby crosswalks in Pride rainbow colors to further acknowledge a once hidden—to mainstream downtown workers anyway—past. Cross Wells Street for **⑰ Real Chili,** one of two locations (both on Wells, 1.5 miles apart) of this iconic chili diner with old-school counter service. Order The Marquette, a medium-spicy chili with spaghetti and beans.

From the diner, take a right (south) on North Jefferson Street, where many upscale bars and eateries line both sides of the street, and then a left (east) on East Mason Street. Another left on North Van Buren Street and a right on East State Street take you past **⑱ The Plaza Hotel** and its Cafe at the Plaza, a favorite of guests and locals alike, open from breakfast to early afternoon.

Continue four blocks on East State Street to North Prospect Avenue. Enter **⑲ Juneau Park,** which is a block south of Walk 16, The East Side (page 90). Keep to the street or walk the paths inside the park, but be sure to note the 1947 replica of Solomon Juneau's cabin, based on a woodcut image of the 1822 original, on the left toward the north end of the park, where East Juneau Avenue begins. To end the walk, keep walking south, back to *The Calling* orange sunburst sculpture in O'Donnell Park.

Points of Interest

① Milwaukee Art Museum 700 N. Art Museum Dr., 414-224-3200, mam.org

② *The Calling* (street art) 929 E. Wisconsin Ave.

③ Betty Brinn Children's Museum 929 E. Wisconsin Ave., 414-390-5437, bbcmkids.org

④ Wisconsin Gas Building (Gas Light Building) 626 E. Wisconsin Ave., wilkow.com/portfolio/gas-light-building

⑤ The Pfister 424 E. Wisconsin Ave., 414-273-8222, thepfisterhotel.com

⑥ Iron Block Building 205 E. Wisconsin Ave.

⑦ City Center at 735 735 N. Water St., citycenter735.com

Juneautown

Points of Interest

8 *OnMilwaukee* 735 N. Water St., Ste. 1120, 414-272-0557, onmilwaukee.com

9 SafeHouse 779 N. Front St., 414-271-2007, safe-house.com

10 Pabst Theater 144 E. Wells St., 414-286-3663 (purchase tickets), 414-286-3205 (direct box office), pabsttheater.org

11 Milwaukee City Hall 200 E. Wells St., 414-286-2489, city.milwaukee.gov

12 Saint Kate 139 E. Kilburn Ave., 414-276-8686, saintkatearts.com

13 Marcus Performing Arts Center 929 N. Water St., 414-273-7206 (box office), marcuscenter.org

14 Milwaukee School of Engineering (MSOE) 1025 N. Broadway, 800-332-6763, msoe.edu

15 Cathedral Square Park 520 E. Wells St., 414-257-7275, countyparks.com

16 This Is It 418 E. Wells St., 414-278-9192, thisisitbar.com

17 Real Chili 419 E. Wells St., 414-271-4042, realchilimilwaukee.com

18 The Plaza Hotel 1007 N. Cass St., 414-276-2101, plazahotelmilwaukee.com

19 Juneau Park 900 N. Prospect Ave., 414-257-7275, countyparks.com, juneauparkfriends.org

2 The Brewery Neighborhood
Old World to New Visions

Above: The patio at Captain Pabst Pilot House

BOUNDARIES: W. Juneau Ave., W. Kilbourn Ave., N. Old World Third St., N. 11th St.
DISTANCE: Approximately 2 miles
DIFFICULTY: Easy
PARKING: In parking structure on Ninth Street or metered parking on surrounding streets
PUBLIC TRANSIT: MCTS route 33 on Winnebago St.

Milwaukee got the nickname Brew City because of its history of beer making (and drinking!) that spans almost two centuries. Companies like Miller, Joseph Schlitz, and Pabst crafted the beers that made Milwaukee famous.

Although Milwaukee doesn't brew as much beer as it did in the past, it continues to contribute to the billion-dollar beer industry. Case in point: Molson Coors (formerly MillerCoors) produces 8.5 million barrels of beer a year. Milwaukee is also home to many local craft breweries, including Lakefront Brewery and the Milwaukee Brewing Company, which is located on this walk.

The walk begins on the grounds of the original Pabst brewery, which closed in 1996, sat vacant for many years, and has recently undergone a transformation. In 2017 the Pabst Milwaukee Brewery and Taproom (now called Captain Pabst Pilot House) opened in the once sprawling compound with a much smaller footprint—in a former church. The redevelopment of this complex inspired the birth of a new neighborhood, The Brewery, that upcycled the once abandoned Pabst buildings into fresh commerce, cuisine, and living concepts.

The Brewery neighborhood is next to a lively section of Milwaukee's downtown known as Westown, which was formerly the settlement Kilbourntown, named after Byron Kilbourn, the city's third founder along with George Walker of Walker's Point and Solomon Juneau, whose settlement was on the east side of the Milwaukee River.

Kilbourn stoked a rivalry with the east side, in essence to gain social and economic superiority for his settlement. That rivalry led to the Bridge War (wherein the Westsiders didn't want bridges connecting the two sides of the river and sabotaged efforts to build and maintain them) and grew so seemingly petty that the street grid was deliberately plotted out differently. This accounts for the odd angles at which downtown Milwaukee's bridges cross the river.

Westown is now an entertainment district that's home to restaurants, bars, popular music venues like Turner Hall, the Milwaukee Public Museum, and the new home of the Milwaukee Bucks, Fiserv Forum.

Walk Description

From the Brewery Parking Structure or the transit stop just beyond, head south on North Ninth Street and take a right on West Juneau Avenue to take in the remaining splendor of the Pabst brewery complex, its sign spanning the street overhead. A mix of transformed brewery buildings and new construction houses a variety of tenants, including the corporate offices of both Milwaukee Film and Klement's Sausage Company; the University of Wisconsin–Milwaukee School of Public Health; Jackson's Blue Ribbon Pub; The Brewhouse Inn & Suites; and Best Place. On the left, ❶ **Best Place at the Historic Pabst Brewery** features a large rental space, a gift shop with the largest selection of beer merchandise in the Midwest, and regular brewery history tours. Among the tour highlights are Captain Frederick Pabst's office and the former brewery's tasting room, where one can indeed get an ice-cold Pabst.

On the next block, ❷ **Jackson's Blue Ribbon Pub** has a house beer, as you can imagine, but also 12 other Wisconsin beers on tap and a full bar, plus a pub fare menu with locally sourced ingredients. Adjacent is ❸ **The Brewhouse Inn & Suites,** which occupies the Pabst brewery's former brewhouse, logically enough, and masterfully incorporates seven gleaming brew kettles into its decor.

The Victorian Gothic building at the end of Juneau on the left was First German Methodist Church In the 1870s and today houses the ❹ **Captain Pabst Pilot House.** Legacy brands such as Andeker are made here, but Pabst is now headquartered in Los Angeles and contracts with Molson Coors to produce its famous Blue Ribbon–winning beer.

Turn left on 11th Street, really just a narrow lane running above the I-43 freeway. The street ends just before Highland Avenue, but the sidewalk continues. Go left on Highland. Trinity Evangelical Lutheran Church was destroyed by a fire that allegedly broke out on the roof during renovations in 2018. The congregation is rebuilding the historic landmark.

Turn left (north) on North Ninth Street. On the left is ❺ **Eleven25,** off-campus student housing located in the former Pabst bottling building. It has a five-restaurant food court that's open to the public.

On the other side of the street, the former Pabst warehouse, Building 42, now houses the ❻ **Glass + Griddle** beer hall and restaurant and two bars, one of which is a rooftop bar, and ❼ **Milwaukee Brewing Company,** a local craft brewery that opened in 1997 in Walker's Point and acquired this space in 2018. They offer six year-round beers, including the flagship brand, an amber ale named Louie's Demise. Tours are available—and highly recommended: "When in Rome, wear a toga; when in Milwaukee, go on a brewery tour."

Turn right and walk east on West Juneau Avenue. At the roundabout, pause to take in the stellar view of the city. ❽ **Fiserv Forum,** the 2018-built, $524 million multipurpose arena that is the home of the Milwaukee Bucks and the Marquette Golden Eagles, looms large ahead on the right. Fiserv hosts roughly 200 events a year, including many large-act concerts and family shows. The 730,000-square-foot arena has 18,000 seats, 34 suites, and three clubs. It's named after Fiserv Inc., a financial services technology company based in Brookfield, a suburb of Milwaukee.

The curved sides of Fiserv Forum are in view as you head east on Juneau Avenue.

Continue toward the forum, crossing North Sixth Street, and walk along the Bucks arena; at the east end, take a right onto the plaza, which is also called Herb Kohl Way, and enter the Deer District, a collection of bars, restaurants, and the Bucks Pro Shop. The Mecca Sports Bar & Grill is named for the former home of the Bucks, and Drink Wisconsinbly is known for its brandy old-fashioned.

❾ **Good City Brewing** joined Milwaukee's craft brewery boom in 2016 and has two locations, the one here and the original on Milwaukee's East Side.

Good City offers year-round canned brews, seasonal cans, and a barrel-aged series in bottles. The brewery also organizes monthly volunteer outings, hosts a podcast called "Speak the Good Podcast," and donates a portion of sales every Thursday to a nonprofit organization.

People gather to watch sporting events outside the forum on a massive outdoor screen. It was particularly popular in the spring of 2019 when the Bucks made it to their first playoff series since 2001. The Bucks advanced to the Eastern Conference Final but lost to the Toronto Raptors.

Walk out of the Deer District plaza and onto North Vel R. Phillips Avenue, where ⑩ **Turner Hall**'s elaborate architecture foreshadows the splendor inside. The 1882 structure is part historic athletic club named for the German American organization American Turners (*turner* means gymnast in German), part restaurant/rental hall, and part magnificent ballroom spanning two stories. Part of The Pabst Theater Group, the ballroom venue hosts live music nightly.

Take a left (east) on West Highland Avenue. ⑪ **Mader's Restaurant,** Milwaukee's oldest restaurant, features old-school German cuisine like schnitzel and sauerbraten (along with lighter, non-German and vegetarian entrées), Bavarian decor, and servers in traditional German attire. The Knights Bar has suits of armor and lots of dark wood and stained glass.

Turn right on Old World Third Street. More German culture is stockpiled across the street at ⑫ **Usinger's,** makers of world-famous German-style smoked sausage and meats. Usinger's opened in 1880 and is run today by the fourth generation of the family. Stop in for free samples and to see the strange and wonderful elf murals.

Keep walking south on Old World Third, past ⑬ **Buck Bradley's Saloon & Eatery,** which features three stories, a main room reminiscent of 1890s Milwaukee beer halls, and the longest bar in the state. The space is a former furniture store built in the mid-1800s with a long, interesting past.

Cross Old World Third at State Street and enter ⑭ **Pere Marquette Park,** which is along the Milwaukee River. The park hosts River Rhythms, a live music event that takes place every Wednesday night during the summer. The beautiful and quite useful Milwaukee County Historical Society building is adjacent to the park.

Turn right on West Kilbourn Avenue. Across the street is the ⑮ **Calderone Club,** a family-owned Milwaukee classic offering Neapolitan-style thin-crust pizza, top-notch Italian dishes like the Penne Salsiccia con Piccante—pasta topped with spicy sausage and made-from-scratch vodka sauce—as well as superb calamari and an extensive wine list. There is a second location in Fox Point, a northern suburb of Milwaukee.

Continue west on West Kilbourn Avenue. While other bars and restaurants have come and gone, ⑯ **Major Goolsby's,** on the right, has stayed in the game for more than 45 years. Its proximity to University of Wisconsin–Milwaukee's Panther Arena, Miller High Life Theatre, and

Wisconsin Center and its commitment to quick service—they have a "Beat the Clock" section on the menu—make it a natural stop before and after games and events. Besides having a simple yet solid menu featuring bratwursts, burgers, wings, and chili, it's also a hangout for famous sports figures and is known for its quirky sense of humor. In the '80s, it hosted a Boy George look-alike contest when Culture Club was playing in town, and much more recently, the bar and restaurant had a huge *Breaking Bad* series-finale viewing party.

On the next block, ⓱ **UW–Milwaukee Panther Arena** is the 12,000-seat home to college basketball, as well as professional ice hockey with the Milwaukee Admirals, flat-track Roller Derby bouts with the Brew City Bruisers, and other events. ⓲ **Miller High Life Theatre,** originally built in 1909 as the Milwaukee Auditorium, seats about 4,000 people and hosts stage performances of all kinds. In 2019, Michelle Obama made a stop at the theater while on her limited-run *Becoming* book tour. Across Kilbourn, ⓳ **Wisconsin Center** hosts conventions and large exhibitions. It has undergone numerous name changes recently, so Milwaukeeans sometimes joke they have no idea what it's called these days.

Turn right (north) on North Sixth Street and then left on West State Street. On the corner is the main building of the downtown campus of ⓴ **Milwaukee Area Technical College (MATC),** a two-year vocational/technical school with 35,000 students and four campuses. The college offers more than 70 associate degrees, including IT, culinary arts, hotel and hospitality management, radiology, and welding technology. In 2018, MATC launched the Promise Program, which offers free tuition to eligible students.

Once back to Ninth Street, hang a right and walk two blocks north to return to the Brewery Parking Structure or public transit just beyond.

Points of Interest

❶ **Best Place at the Historic Pabst Brewery** 917 W. Juneau Ave., 414-630-1609, bestplacemilwaukee.com

❷ **Jackson's Blue Ribbon Pub** 1203 N. 10th St., 414-276-7271, jacksonsmke.com

❸ **The Brewhouse Inn & Suites** 1215 N. 10th St., 414-810-3350, brewhousesuites.com

❹ **Captain Pabst Pilot House** 1037 W. Juneau Ave., 414-908-0025, captainpabst1864.com /pages/pilot-house

❺ **The Restaurants at Eleven25** 1125 N. Ninth St., 414-376-7300

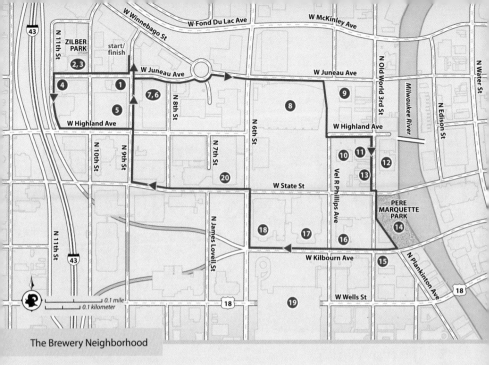

The Brewery Neighborhood

6 **Glass + Griddle** 1130 N. Ninth St., 414-988-1551, glassgriddle.com

7 **Milwaukee Brewing Company** 1128 N. Ninth St., 414-226-2337, mkebrewing.com

8 **Fiserv Forum** 1111 Vel R. Phillips Ave., 414-227-0504, fiservforum.com

9 **Good City Brewing** 333 W. Juneau Ave., 414-539-4343, goodcitybrewing.com

10 **Turner Hall** 1040 Vel R. Phillips Ave.; 414-286-3663 (purchase tickets), 414-286-3205 (direct box office); pabsttheater.org/venue/turner-hall-ballroom

11 **Mader's Restaurant** 1041 N. Old World Third St., 414-271-3377, madersrestaurant.com

12 **Usinger's** 1030 N. Old World Third St., 414-276-9100, usinger.com

13 **Buck Bradley's Saloon & Eatery** 1019 N. Old World Third St., 414-224-8500, buckbradleys.com

14 **Pere Marquette Park** 900 N. Plankinton Ave., 414-257-7275, countyparks.com

15 **Calderone Club** 842 N. Old World Third St., 414-273-3236, calderoneclub.net

16 **Major Goolsby's** 340 W. Kilbourn Ave., 414-271-3414, majorgoolsbys.com

17 **UW–Milwaukee Panther Arena** 400 W. Kilbourn Ave., 414-908-6000, uwmilwaukeepantherarena.com

18 **Miller High Life Theatre** 500 W. Kilbourn Ave., 414-908-6000, millerhighlifetheatre.com

19 **Wisconsin Center** 400 W. Wisconsin Ave., 414-908-6000, wisconsincenter.com

20 **Milwaukee Area Technical College (MATC)** 700 W. State St., 414-297-6282, matc.edu

3 Third Ward
Where Art, Fashion, and Nature Meet

BOUNDARIES: E. Saint Paul Ave., E. Erie St., Milwaukee Bay, Milwaukee River
DISTANCE: Approximately 3.5 miles
DIFFICULTY: Easy
PARKING: Street parking or the Milwaukee Public Market pay lot
PUBLIC TRANSIT: MCTS routes 15 and the Green Line; The Hop streetcar stops along Saint Paul Avenue at S. Water St.

The Historic Third Ward, located directly south of downtown, is Milwaukee's oldest center of commerce and warehousing that continues to bustle as a retail, entertainment, residential, and arts district.

It is also possibly Milwaukee's most resilient neighborhood. In 1892, The Great Third Ward Fire destroyed almost the entire neighborhood, but within 30 years it was completely rebuilt.

Currently the Third Ward boasts more than 500 businesses, including restaurants, fashion boutiques, theater groups, specialty shops, art and photography studios, advertising agencies, graphic artists, and roughly 20 art galleries.

The neighborhood is also the home to the Milwaukee Institute of Art and Design (MIAD) and the Broadway Theatre Center, which houses the world-renowned Skylight Music Theatre, Renaissance Theatreworks, and Milwaukee Chamber Theatre and hosts the quarterly Gallery Night & Day event.

The neighborhood also includes the Henry W. Maier Festival Park, which for more than 50 years has hosted Summerfest, the world's largest outdoor music festival, as well as numerous ethnic festivals, concerts, political gatherings, and more.

Walk Description

Enter the ❶ **Milwaukee Public Market** from South Water Street. Check out food, drink, and local shopping. Opened in 2005, the market is one of the neighborhood's anchor establishments with roughly 18 vendors offering everything from Thai cuisine to local coffee to fresh lobster. It's also Milwaukee Souvenir Heaven with tasteful and fun items representing Brew City (translation: no foam cheese-head hats). Exit from the east end of the market, out the doors just past the Saint Paul Fish Company (awesome lobster rolls), and step onto North Broadway.

Head south to cross East Saint Paul Avenue at the light. On the corner is ❷ **The Wicked Hop**, a zillion-time winner in best Bloody Mary contests around the city (three words: cheese whip garnish). The bar and restaurant's name is derived from a baseball term used when a batter hits a sharp ground ball that seems like an easy out but unexpectedly bounces in another direction. This happened in game one of the 1982 World Series—the only World Series attended by the Milwaukee Brewers—helping the Brewers clinch a 10-0 victory. Before moving on, glance down Broadway, where bustling local retail and dining spots are peppered with national chains such as Anthropologie and Warby Parker. Note the amazing awnings on the buildings in this warehouse district as they stretch out to meet the street. You can almost imagine the horse-drawn wagons backed up to buildings underneath, loading and unloading wares.

From The Wicked Hop, head west on East Saint Paul Avenue. Local coffee chain Colectivo has a café here. Take a left on N. Water Street.

At the southeast corner of the next intersection is the ❸ **Marshall Building,** a century-old warehouse, like so many in this part of the neighborhood, that now holds commercial and retail spaces; a good Chinese restaurant (Jing's); studios and galleries, like Portrait Society Gallery; and on the third floor, the Too Much Metal for One Hand showroom for more Milwaukee-themed clothing.

Across Water Street in a stretch of other bars and restaurants is the Milwaukee Ale House, where Milwaukee Brewing Company got its start. The Royal Enfield motorcycle dealership is on your left and then Gouda's Italian Deli, which is a "front" for ❹ **Bugsy's Back Alley Speakeasy**, a Prohibition-themed cocktail lounge accessible from the alley behind Gouda's.

Take a left on East Chicago Street. At the next intersection is the ❺ **Kimpton Journeyman** hotel, which is committed to incorporating local art on the walls and in the decor, and also contains The Outsider, its ninth-floor restaurant and bar with a stunning view.

Turn right on North Broadway. The ❻ **Broadway Theatre Center** is at the end of the block and houses two unique theaters: the Cabot Theatre, a replica of an 18th-century European opera house, and the intimate "black box" Studio Theatre. Performing companies include the Skylight Music Theatre, Milwaukee Chamber Theatre, and Renaissance Theaterworks.

Note the historical marker for the Third Ward Fire of 1892 across Menomonee Street and walk into the small park called Catalano Square. The massive piece of bubblegum-colored public art is *The Pink Planet,* named for the planet discovered by NASA in 2013.

Cross the park to East Erie Street. The ❼ **Milwaukee Institute of Art and Design (MIAD)** stands across Erie southwest of the park. MIAD is a four-year, private college offering Bachelor of Fine Arts degrees in a number of disciplines.

Turn left (southeast) on Erie Street. Upscale condos along the river have drawn older suburbanites back to the city, as have a couple of restaurants just beyond a slight bend in the road. The first is Riverfront Pizzeria, which abuts the recently developed ❽ **Trestle Park,** city property built atop a trestle that extends into the river toward a swing bridge. No longer used, but still owned by Union Pacific Railroad, the bridge remains open for water traffic to pass on the river below.

Follow Erie Street 0.25 mile to where it curves left along the Kinnickinnic River. As you walk east on a leg of the Hank Aaron State Trail, Lake Michigan is ahead. The Daniel Hoan Bridge, affectionately nicknamed by Milwaukeeans as simply The Hoan, is the bright yellow structure towering above you. Named after one of Milwaukee's Socialist mayors, The Hoan is part of the I-794 freeway, and was also sometimes referred to as The Bridge to Nowhere by people who either have a low opinion of Bay View, which lies beyond, or just don't like public works projects. While still under construction, the freeway was featured in the 1980 film classic starring Dan Aykroyd and John Belushi, *The Blues Brothers.*

While walking under The Hoan, keep your eyes on the red lighthouse between you and Lake Michigan. Officially named ❾ **Milwaukee Pierhead Light,** the little cardinal-tinted tower marks the inlet to Milwaukee's inner harbor.

Go left (north) and continue on the street or the paths along Lake Michigan, often lined with people fishing from the pier in all kinds of weather. That big hill to your left is actually the American

Family Insurance Amphitheater on the Summerfest grounds. The street ends, but well-kept paths continue to **⑩ Lakeshore State Park,** 22 acres of sand and restored native grasses with a winding, easily walkable trail and incredible views of the city and the lake. The park is open daily from 6 a.m. to 10 p.m. As you walk the paths to the northern end, consider how all this apparent natural beauty exists on top of earthen debris drilled from underneath the city when the Milwaukee Metropolitan Sewerage District (MMSD) built the Deep Tunnel, which is actually a system of tunnels stretching more than 28 miles at 135–300 feet belowground. According to MMSD, the Deep Tunnel project has kept more than 124 billion gallons of pollution from entering Lake Michigan.

Exit Lakeshore State Park, continuing on the Hank Aaron State Trail paths along Milwaukee Bay. The north end of the Summerfest grounds is right alongside you and **⑪ Discovery World** is ahead on the right. The science and technology museum focuses on the ecology of the Great Lakes, and its many interactive exhibits are entertaining and educational for explorers of all ages.

Take a left, walking west away from the lake, on East Clybourn Street. This is the northern border of the Historic Third Ward. Often changing, this area is experiencing enormous growth and new construction. Downtown Milwaukee's main financial and commercial district is to the right, the mostly elevated I-794 to your left. After the interstate touches down near the north gate to Henry Maier Festival Park, it takes off again to the south and up over the Hoan Bridge.

After about 300 feet, take a left on North Harbor Drive, which after a short walk curves right and ends at North Lincoln Memorial Drive. Take a left. All the parking lots surrounding you are for the festival grounds, and its stages are visible over the fencing on the left.

The impossible-to-miss main entrance to the Henry W. Maier Festival Park, often referred to simply as the **⑫ Summerfest** grounds, stands out at the intersection with Chicago Street. Summerfest—aka The Big Gig—is an 11-day, world-renowned music festival held every summer along the lakefront. The festival grounds also host myriad ethnic festivals, including Festa Italiana, Mexican Fiesta, German Fest, and Indian Summer Festival.

Take a right (west) on East Chicago Street. Note **⑬ The Italian Community Center** and its shiny *New Beginnings* statue, erected in 2019 and dedicated to immigrants of all races and nationalities who came to America.

Henry W. Maier Festival Park, home of the annual Summerfest music festival

Turn left (south) on North Jackson Street. Apartments and retail are to your right, and parking lots for the community center and Summerfest are to your left. In one of the structures is Camp Bar, which also has locations in two Milwaukee suburbs.

The Baumgartner Center for Dance, completed in 2019, stands at the end of Jackson Street. The new home of the **14** **Milwaukee Ballet,** the 52,000-square-foot building has seven studios, seating for 200, and the latest in ballet flooring technology.

Turn right on East Corcoran Street. There are more warehouses and loading docks to see, seemingly permanent monuments to the Third Ward's commercial past. Take a right on North Jefferson Street and then a left on East Menomonee Street. Catalano Square will make a brief appearance again. Across from the square on Menomonee is **15** **Bavette La Boucherie,** a contemporary, woman-owned butcher shop offering all sustainable meats with an on-site café.

If that doesn't tempt you to cross the street and head inside, take a right on North Milwaukee Street. Bella Caffé, which has excellent soups, is at the next intersection. Music recording facilities, workout gyms, law offices, and more art galleries line the street. At the northwest corner of the next intersection is **16** **MODA3,** a hip, locally owned streetwear store that's been in business for over 15 years. It is located inside the historic 1922 P.H. Dye House, originally a Phoenix Hosiery Company's dyeing plant. Note the massive north-facing wall mural of the headless woman in the apron. The model for the mural is chef Karen Bell, who owns Bavette La Boucherie, and was painted by a German artist in 2019 as a tribute to working women in the Third Ward neighborhood. Milwaukeeans are mixed in their feelings about this mural. What do you think?

Across the street are two beloved food spots, Holey Moley—a specialty doughnut joint—and Smoke Shack, a favorite barbecue restaurant among locals. (Oh, the brisket!)

Turn left on East Saint Paul Avenue. On the right before returning to the Public Market, check out the **17** **Commission House.** The 1911 building is now home to condos and commercial units, but over the years stored fruit, fish, church missals, and accordions. A "ghost sign" for Lo Duca Bros. Inc.—the accordion manufacturers and wine distributors who owned the building until 2002—remains on the north side of the building.

Points of Interest

1 **Milwaukee Public Market** 400 N. Water St., 414-336-1111, milwaukeepublicmarket.org

2 **The Wicked Hop** 345 N. Broadway, 414-223-0345, thewickedhop.com

3 **Marshall Building** 207 E. Buffalo St., 414-276-5210, marshallbuildingmke.com

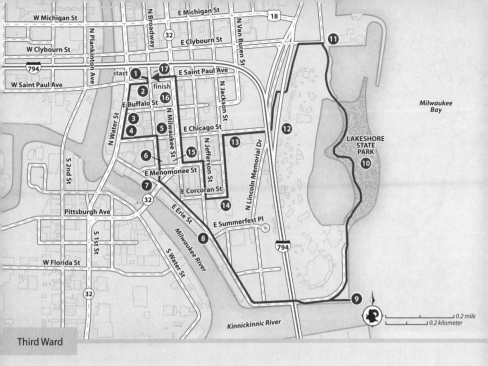

④ **Bugsy's Back Alley Speakeasy** 218 N. Water St., 414-221-6564, bugsysmke.com

⑤ **Kimpton Journeyman** 310 E. Chicago St., 414-291-3970, journeymanhotel.com

⑥ **Broadway Theatre Center** 158 N. Broadway, 414-291-7800, broadwaytheatrecenter.com

⑦ **Milwaukee Institute of Art and Design (MIAD)** 273 E. Erie St., 888-749-6423, miad.edu

⑧ **Trestle Park** 501 E. Erie St.

⑨ **Milwaukee Pierhead Light** East end of East Erie Street

⑩ **Lakeshore State Park** 500 N. Harbor Drive, 414-274-4281, dnr.wi.gov/topic/parks/name/lakeshore

⑪ **Discovery World** 500 N. Harbor Drive, 414-765-9966, discoveryworld.org

⑫ **Summerfest** 639 E. Summerfest Place, 414-273-2680, summerfest.com

⑬ **The Italian Community Center** 631 E. Chicago St., 414-223-2180, iccmilwaukee.com

⑭ **Milwaukee Ballet** 128 N. Jackson St., 414-902-2103 (tickets), 414-643-7677 (general), milwaukeeballet.org

⑮ **Bavette La Boucherie** 330 E. Menomonee St., 414-273-3375, bavettelaboucherie.com

⑯ **MODA3** 320 E. Buffalo St., 414-273-3333, www.moda3.com

⑰ **Commission House** (private residences) 400 N. Broadway

4 Upper East Side
Eat, Drink, and Declare Your Major

Above: The historic Goldberg Mansion on East Newberry Boulevard

BOUNDARIES: E. Hartford Ave., E. Webster Pl., North Lake Dr., N. Newhall St.
DISTANCE: Approximately 3.75 miles
DIFFICULTY: Easy
PARKING: Street parking or public lot west of Urban Ecology Center
PUBLIC TRANSIT: MCTS Green Line is on Oakland.

Since the 1960s, "the East Side" in general is synonymous to locals with all that is hip, trendy, and progressive. In later decades, other modern and dynamic neighborhoods materialized, but the East Side will always have its cred for being über cool.

Because it's on the bluff above Lake Michigan, the eclectic East Side is literally and figuratively "cooler by the lake." It consists of quintessential neighborhoods ideal for a romantic date night, a casual dinner and a film, bar hopping, or a contemplative walk with spontaneous stops at bookshops and cafés.

This particular walk covers the Upper East Side, the far-northeast end of the area; just beyond University of Wisconsin–Milwaukee's (UWM's) main campus is the suburb of Shorewood. In addition to the university, the walk encompasses one of three Urban Ecology Centers in the city, two parks (both of which were designed by Frederick Law Olmsted, who created New York's Central Park), many residential communities, and multiple business and dining districts.

Although students now occupy many of the homes around campus, the Upper East Side has a large population of longtime residents and homeowners, including Italian immigrants and descendants, who have contributed some of the most beloved eateries, markets, and bakeries to the city. The result is a fresh, eclectic, and vibrant area that's highly coveted by Milwaukeeans looking for either a stable neighborhood or a fun night out.

Walk Description

Start walking east on East Park Place. On the left, the ❶ **Urban Ecology Center–Riverside Park (UEC)** sits atop the Milwaukee River bluff and overlooks the popular Oak Leaf Trail. There are three UECs in Milwaukee, all of which have the mission to "connect people in cities to nature and each other." The organization does this through educating the community about the environment, conservation, sustainability, and other issues related to urban ecology. A trip to the top of the observation tower is highly recommended.

Pass by Milwaukee Fire Department station 27 and cross busy North Oakland Avenue. Two blocks ahead is ❷ **Outwords Books, Gifts & Coffee,** a full-service bookstore and gift shop with an LGBTQ emphasis that has been serving the community for over 20 years.

Turn left (north) on North Murray Avenue and then right on East Newberry Boulevard. Newberry Boulevard's 12 blocks are a lasting artifact of the City Beautiful movement, whose proponents at the end of the 19th century insisted that a city should improve the aesthetic environment for its residents.

Be sure to find the "castle"—or Historic Goldberg Mansion—at 2727 E. Newberry, a couple of blocks past Downer Avenue. Even among the ostentation of the area, this Châteauesque-style home stands out. Built in 1896 by a lawyer who was disbarred, ran out of money, and couldn't finish its construction, the mansion was among the first in its newly platted subdivision and features seven bedrooms, three and a half bathrooms, a carriage house (with another bathroom), a butler's pantry—whatever the rich needed to feel as such, this home's got it.

Dipping down into one of the area's commercial districts requires an interruption of the tour of big homes. Take a right on North Downer Avenue (if you passed Downer to see the Goldberg Mansion, you'll need to backtrack).

This stretch of Downer Avenue has been a hub of film, food, literature, and fashion since the 1950s. Lifelong Milwaukeeans reminisce about the long-defunct Coffee Trader, now ❸ **BelAir Cantina,** a local chain of six Mexican eateries known for mix-and-match street tacos and good margaritas. However, history remains intact with old-school haunts still in operation like The Downer Theater, Sendik's Food Market, and Henry's, which changed locations on the block but has been tapping beers since 1982.

Milwaukee's beloved ❹ **Pizza Man** relocated to Downer Avenue after the original location on North Avenue burned down in 2010. Although some say the new location can't compete with the lovable quirkiness of the old restaurant that included small booths made of wood and a locally famous bright-yellow sign that many described as "phallic shaped," the new location does sport an incredible second floor with balcony seating and a menu that offers new options like cauliflower-crust pies along with institutions like the spicy meatball and the artichoke à la mode.

"New" favorites on the street include ❺ **Boswell Book Company,** a locally owned indie bookstore that assumed the corner space in 2008 after the former bookshop of 82 years, Harry W. Schwartz Booksellers, closed its doors. The adjoining café, now a Starbucks, was a popular hangout spot for young professionals, college students, skaters, and "alternative" teens in the '80s and '90s called Brewster's and later Webster's Cafe.

Exiting Boswell, take a left (north) back up the street and then a right on East Belleview Place, only to turn immediately left on North Hackett Avenue, which hits the intersection at an angle. Hackett straightens out after the first block and its two churches. Go another block due north and return to the big houses of East Newberry Boulevard.

Take a right (east) and walk three blocks. At North Lake Drive, note Lake Park across the street (here, you can also join the Lakefront walk, page 84). Turn left on Lake and walk three blocks north to East Kenwood Boulevard.

Take a left on Kenwood, walk five more mostly residential blocks, and arrive at the ❻ **University of Wisconsin–Milwaukee (UWM).** A Carnegie R1 research institution and the second-largest in the state system after the University of Wisconsin–Madison, UWM has 15 schools and colleges, including the state's only schools of architecture, public health, and freshwater sciences, which is located in the city's Harbor District. The film school at UWM's Peck School of the Arts is consistently named one of the world's best.

The observation tower at the Urban Ecology Center in Riverside Park

Take a right (north) on North Downer Avenue. Campus buildings are on both sides of the street along with some eating establishments and other businesses on the right, including **7** **Sala,** a neighborhood classic. Chef Anthony Balistreri and his sister Teresa opened the restaurant focusing on Sicilian cuisine when they were both in their early 20s.

Across the street is **8** **Mitchell Hall,** formerly the site of the Milwaukee State Normal School (a training site for teachers) and then the Milwaukee State Teachers College, the precursor to UWM. The brutalist-style structure next door is Curtin Hall, home to many humanities, language, and philosophy programs, and creates a stark contrast with surrounding buildings.

Turn left on East Hartford Avenue. **9** **Golda Meir Library** is the central building for many libraries and collections. Named after the former prime minister of Israel, Ukrainian immigrant Meir also lived and studied in Milwaukee, including at the State Normal School in 1916. Easy to study or get lost in, the fourth-floor Special Collections area of rare books and materials is particularly worth spending an hour in—or a week.

Cross the busy intersection at Maryland Avenue with a thousand or so college students to enter the decidedly more science-oriented part of campus. The colleges of health sciences and nursing are located here, along with chemistry, engineering, and the newer Kenwood Interdisciplinary Research Complex. UWM's internationally renowned School of Architecture and Urban Planning is on the corner.

Continue walking west off campus and turn left onto North Cramer Street. With residential housing to the right and the campus still to the left. A block down is UWM's **10** **Manfred Olson**

Planetarium, named after the longtime UWM physics professor. With often themed public shows and special events, the planetarium has drawn college students, school groups, and the public alike into astronomy and the beauty of the cosmos for over 50 years.

Turn right on East Kenwood Boulevard, go one block, then turn left on North Oakland Avenue. Walking south, note the numerous iconic local restaurants in this commercial strip built up because of both university and neighborhood traffic. ⓫ **Lisa's Pizzeria** was opened by Joseph Bongiorno in 1960 (Lisa is one of his nieces) and is often filled with neighborhood regulars. The Italian sausage is made in-house. The pizza crust is an example of a classic Milwaukee thin, crackery crust, which isn't always easy to identify. Saying any thin crust is particular to Milwaukee is a matter of knowing it when you have it; fortunately, there are a lot of thin crusts to be had in Milwaukee to help you build up this understanding.

Founded in 1948, ⓬ **George Webb** is part of a classic chain of Wisconsin diners known for giving away free burgers when the Brewers win 10 games in a row (it has happened twice in history) and for having two identical clocks on the walls. The clocks were a result of a city ordinance prohibiting 24-hour establishments, coupled with the founder's sense of humor. Webb declared that his restaurants were open "23 hours, 59 minutes, and 59 seconds, seven days a week and on Sundays." The clocks were set one minute apart to demonstrate the opening and closing times.

The intersection of Oakland Avenue and Locust Street is one of the East Side's busiest corners and is responsible for the "Oak & Loc" tagline for that part of the neighborhood. ⓭ **Oakland Gyros** is a staple on this corner of otherwise changing sandwich shops and burger joints for the college crowd. Dive bar enthusiasts will want to check out ⓮ **Axel's Inn**—popular among college students, particularly English majors, as well as neighborhood locals.

Keep walking south, alongside ⓯ **Riverside Park.** A detour through the park is encouraged, as your destination, the Urban Ecology Center, is visible on a crest in the distance with doors that open up to the park. Otherwise, take a right on East Riverside Place and a left on North Bartlett Avenue. Take another right at the edge of the park on East Park Place to return to the start.

You'll find classic Milwaukee thin-crust pizza at Lisa's Pizzeria.

Points of Interest

1. **Urban Ecology Center–Riverside Park** 1500 E. Park Place, 414-964-8505, urbanecologycenter.org
2. **Outwords Books, Gifts & Coffee** 2710 N. Murray Ave., 414-963-9089, outwordsbooks.com
3. **BelAir Cantina** 2625 N. Downer Ave., 414-964-1190, belaircantina.com
4. **Pizza Man** 2597 N. Downer Ave., 414-272-1745, pizzamanwi.com
5. **Boswell Book Company** 2559 N. Downer Ave., 414-332-1181, boswellbooks.com
6. **University of Wisconsin–Milwaukee** 2100 E. Kenwood Blvd., 414-229-1122, uwm.edu
7. **Sala** 2613 E. Hampshire St., 414-964-2611, saladining.com
8. **Mitchell Hall** (formerly State Normal School), 3203 N. Downer Ave., uwm.edu/search/locations/MIT
9. **Gold Meir Library** 2311 E. Hartford Ave., 414-229-4785, uwm.edu/libraries
10. **Manfred Olson Planetarium** 1900 E. Kenwood Blvd., 414-229-4961, uwm.edu/planetarium
11. **Lisa's Pizzeria** 2961 N. Oakland Ave., 414-332-6360, pizzabylisa.com
12. **George Webb** 2935 N. Oakland Ave., 414-332-6044, georgewebb.com
13. **Oakland Gyros** 2867 N. Oakland Ave., 414-963-1393
14. **Axel's Inn** 2859 N. Oakland Ave., 414-962-2122
15. **Riverside Park** 1500 E. Riverside Place, 414-257-7275, countyparks.com

5 Bronzeville
Jazz and Justice

Above: Milwaukee Fire Station No. 21 in Brewer's Hill, a neighborhood known for its architecture

BOUNDARIES: E. North Ave., W. Pleasant St., N. Hubbard St., N. Fifth St.
DISTANCE: Approximately 2.25 miles
DIFFICULTY: Medium (slight slope gradations along the route)
PARKING: Street parking on MLK Dr.
PUBLIC TRANSIT: MCTS routes 19 on MLK Dr. and 57 on Walnut St.

In some important ways, Bronzeville is more a state of mind than a particular neighborhood. The organization Visit Milwaukee calls Bronzeville "the historic economic and social heart of Milwaukee's African American community." But that history was centered on a geographical area that was forever transformed in the 1960s by freeway construction and subsequent city planning, which ripped the social fabric of this grand old neighborhood apart.

There is indeed a recent city-backed redevelopment area called Bronzeville that extends over parts of what is now the Halyard Park and Brewer's Hill neighborhoods. Other initiatives include parts of neighboring Hillside and Harambee. Each of these areas have their own histories and distinct identities, but taken together, and with an open acknowledgment of history and a strong desire to build a future, a new and exciting Bronzeville is in fact coalescing.

One of the oldest parts of the city, the area was developed by German immigrants in the 1850s, and by 1900 was mostly home to increasing numbers of African Americans and newcomers from Eastern Europe, including many Jewish immigrants.

After World War II, Bronzeville flourished when thousands of black Southerners came to live and secure factory jobs or open family businesses in Milwaukee. By 1950, Milwaukee's black community grew to 20,000 and old Bronzeville was at its pinnacle of prosperity, with 180 black-owned businesses, including restaurants, record stores, department stores, barbershops, jewelers, the opulent Regal Theater, and scads of nationally known jazz clubs that attracted big names like Billie Holiday, Duke Ellington, Count Basie, Dizzy Gillespie, and Nat King Cole.

Today, with the city-backed initiatives, including The Bronzeville Cultural and Entertainment District, the area is attracting young, local entrepreneurs who infuse new energy with history and are working hard to build new lives in the area. In recent years, a redevelopment initiative began to celebrate the past and nurture the strong roots of jazz and the arts, with festivals, gallery shows, and other cultural events. The neighborhoods are once again home to numerous African American–owned businesses, restaurants, and art collectives.

Many parts of Bronzeville are known for old structures—Brewer's Hill in particular for having large Victorian homes on spacious lots. Brewer's Hill is a diverse neighborhood with new condo and restaurant concepts popping up with increasing regularity, whereas Halyard Park has a unique, almost peculiar, suburban feel and is home to many middle-class African American families. Hillside, just to the south, remains predominantly composed of the working class and poor.

Walk Description

Start at the ❶ statue of Dr. Martin Luther King Jr. on the east side of N. Dr. Martin Luther King Jr. Drive just south of Vine Street. The bronze statue, created by artist Erik Blome, features Dr. King speaking while standing on a stack of books.

Across the street at the next intersection, West Reservoir Avenue, is the ❷ Benedict Center, a nonprofit organization that helps women and their children with substance abuse, mental health treatment, education, and support in the prison system. It also offers programs to aid women who are homeless or working in prostitution.

Walk north, crossing Reservoir Avenue and Brown Street, to get to some seemingly permanent fixtures in this commercial district, such as ❸ Fein Brothers, a food-service equipment and supply dealer that opened in 1929 and moved to its current location in 1967. Its King Drive showroom with that huge midcentury sign is open to the public and stocks more than 60,000 food service items in the multilevel store. Anyone need a spatula?

Next door is ❹ DreamBikes, a nonprofit with five locations nationwide: three in Wisconsin, one in New York, and one in Tennessee. They open used bicycle stores in low- to moderate-income neighborhoods to provide training and paid jobs to teens, who learn how to refurbish bicycles, perform quality customer service, use point-of-sale software, and more. DreamBikes is open to the public and sells bikes at affordable prices. Since 2008, DreamBikes has repurposed more than 10,000 bikes.

Across the street, ❺ Crown Hardware and Plumbing Supply is an old-school holdout in an era of big-box stores. Customers travel from around the city for the employees' decades' worth of expertise. Just a few doors down are also Northern Chocolate Co. and ❻ Adambomb Gallerie. Adambomb was Milwaukee's first tattoo shop to open after tattooing became legal in Milwaukee again in 1997. The owner and many past employees are graduates of the Milwaukee Institute of Art and Design (MIAD), in the city's Third Ward (see Walk 3, page 14).

At West Lloyd Street, take a left and head into the Halyard Park neighborhood. Halyard Park is a subdivision that purposefully looks and feels like a tract of single-family, suburban-style homes. Follow Lloyd as it curves right (north), becoming North Fifth Street.

Beechie Brooks, a community leader and real estate developer with a vision to revitalize the central city, developed the neighborhood in the 1970s and named it after Ardie and Wilbur Halyard, a husband-and-wife team who founded Columbia Savings and Loan in 1924. The bank was established to provide mortgage loans to Milwaukee's African American community. Today Halyard Park is a small, tight-knit neighborhood committed to peace and community.

Community is demonstrated daily on the next corner at ❼ Garfield's 502, a bar, restaurant, and neighborhood staple that draws people from all over the city and is the latest iteration

See old Victorian-style homes as you walk down Palmer Street in Brewer's Hill.

of black-owned establishments in that location since 1955. Sometimes still referred to as Boobie's, after a previous owner who put his nickname on the place, Garfield's is actually that former space and two others on the corner, which current owner Jewel Currie brought together with his business partner. While all the food is good at Garfield's, we recommend trying the catfish and fried okra.

Take a right on West Garfield Avenue and a left on North Vel R. Phillips Avenue. This street, formerly North Fourth Street, was renamed in 2018 after Velvalea Hortense Rodgers "Vel" Phillips, an attorney, politician, and civil rights activist who also served as an alderwoman, a judge, and Wisconsin's secretary of state. Trailblazing Phillips was often both the first woman and the first African American in her many positions.

8 **America's Black Holocaust Museum** is on the next corner in new construction connected to the former Garfield Avenue public school, which is now apartments (be sure to check out the north-facing mural when you reach this building). It's the second location for the museum and was scheduled to open in 2020. The original museum, dedicated in 1988 to the victims of racial violence and oppression, was founded by James Cameron, the United States' only known survivor of a lynching. Through exhibits, events, lectures, and more, the museum raises public awareness of the unforgivable acts and aftermath of American slavery and works to promote racial repair, reconciliation, and healing.

Take a right (east) on West North Avenue. On the northeast corner of the next intersection, the Wisconsin Department of Natural Resources offices are housed in a reclaimed bank building. On the northwest corner stands **9** **Pete's Fruit Market,** one of two Pete's locations in Milwaukee—the other is on the Chavez walk (page 78). When this location opened in 2018, it provided a much-needed grocery store in the area. Pete's is known for its fresh, affordable, and specialty produce that's bundled into baskets like at a farmers market. Pete's also partnered with the City of Milwaukee and local organizations to create a community farm.

Turn right (south) on North Dr. Martin Luther King Jr. Drive. The next block holds new art studios, beauty supply stores, and the Skybox Sports Bar on the west side, and on the east, **10** **Gee's Clippers.** Gaulien Smith originally opened the barber shop in the Sherman Park neighborhood in 1995. His King Drive shop is a former bank with a full basketball court and 72 chairs in the waiting area that were taken from the former Bucks arena, known as The Mecca, downtown. Smith grew up on Milwaukee's north side and started cutting his own hair when he was a kid and, as he improved, also cut his siblings' and friends' hair. Now a barber instructor, Smith also cuts Bucks players' hair in their training facility across from the new arena, Fiserv Forum (Walk 2, page 8).

Take a left (east) on West Garfield Avenue and head into the Historic Brewer's Hill neighborhood. Named after the large number of brewery workers and owners who once inhabited the area, Brewer's Hill features storybook-inspired Victorians, many of which are strikingly painted, as well as many smaller homes. The neighborhood suffered a decline in the 1960s and '70s, when it lost many businesses and residents. By 1981, however, the area was on the upswing again.

Pass by ⓫ **Mount Zion Missionary Baptist Church** on the left and the Calvin Courtyard Apartments affordable housing on the right. A neighborhood bulwark, Mount Zion celebrated its 100th year in 2018.

In two blocks, take a right on North Palmer Street. You'll start to notice a greater proliferation of old Victorian-style dwellings. Even public-service buildings are old and ornate here: Milwaukee Fire Station No. 21 was built in 1894.

Turn right (west) on East Brown Street and left (south) on North First Street. On the left is George Washington Carver Academy, a public school named after the famous scientist. A park just west of this walk was also renamed to recognize him.

Take a left (east) on East Reservoir Avenue and a right (south) to return to North Palmer Street. The ⓬ **Sanger House Gardens** is an event space and bed-and-breakfast with a storied past, including as the home of Milwaukee mayor Joseph Phillips. According to Milwaukee historian John Gurda, among other sources, the Sanger House was purchased in 1975 by bricklayer Ron Radke, who spent the next 10 years restoring it. As an "urban pioneer," notes Gurda, Radke launched the preservationist movement in the neighborhood.

Turn left (east) on East Vine Street. At the end of the block is View MKE; this rehabbed space housed one of the first new restaurants in the neighborhood. On the northwest corner is ⓭ **Uncle Wolfie's Breakfast Tavern,** a bar and restaurant inside a spectacular building that was once a Miller Brewing Company tied house (meaning it was under contract to buy from Miller). Uncle Wolfie's is open for breakfast, brunch, and lunch. There are plenty of cocktails—including Bloody Marys, mimosas, and drinks made with coffee or tea—to start the day off right. The house specialty is called the BELTCH, a breakfast sandwich stacked with bacon, eggs, lettuce, tomatoes, and cheddar. Try to order it without smirking.

Take a right (south) on North Hubbard Street. From this vantage on the bluff above the Milwaukee River are splendid views of the city. Turn left to walk south on Palmer briefly before turning right on East Pleasant Street. Note ⓮ **Schlitz Park** across the street, technically its own neighborhood (one with no residents) and the former home of the massive Joseph Schlitz Brewing Company. "The beer that made Milwaukee famous" was first brewed in 1849. Commercial tenants—most of them corporate headquarters—now occupy the remaining five buildings.

In three blocks, take a final right (north) back on Dr. Martin Luther King Jr. Drive and return to the MLK statue.

Bronzeville

Points of Interest

1. **Statue of Dr. Martin Luther King Jr.** Between 1724 and 1740 N. Dr. Martin Luther King Jr. Drive

2. **Benedict Center** 1849 N. Dr. Martin Luther King Jr. Drive, 414-347-1774, benedictcenter.org

3. **Fein Brothers** 2007 N. Dr. Martin Luther King Jr. Drive, 414-562-0220, feinbrothers.com

4. **Dream Bikes** 2021 N. Martin Luther King Jr. Drive, 414-763-0909, dream-bikes.org

5. **Crown Hardware and Plumbing Supply** 2016 N. Martin Luther King Jr. Drive, 414-374-5100, crownhardwareandplumbing.com

6. **Adambomb Gallerie** 2028 N. Dr. Martin Luther King Jr. Drive., 414-881-8020, adambombgallerie.com

7. **Garfield's 502** 502 W. Garfield Ave., 414-374-4502, garfields502.com

8. **America's Black Holocaust Museum** 401 W. North Ave., 414-209-3640, www.abhmuseum.org

9. **Pete's Fruit Market** 2323 N. Dr. Martin Luther King Jr. Drive, 414-383-1300, petesfruitmarket.com

10. **Gee's Clippers** 2200 N. Dr. Martin Luther King Jr. Drive, 414-442-7588, geesclippers.com

11. **Mount Zion Missionary Baptist Church** 2207 N. Second St., 414-372-7811, mtzmke.org

12. **Sanger House Gardens** 1823 N. Palmer St., 414-640-6003, sangerhousegardens.com

13. **Uncle Wolfie's Breakfast Tavern** 234 E. Vine St., 414-763-3021, unclewolfies.com

14. **Schlitz Park** Intersection of West Pleasant and North Second Streets, schlitzpark.com

6 Bluemound Heights
It Must Be the Custard

Above: Maxie's serves Southern comfort food, barbecue, seafood, and Bourbon Street favorites.

BOUNDARIES: W. Bluemound Rd., W. Fairview Ave., N. Hawley Rd., N. 76th St.
DISTANCE: Approximately 3.25 miles
DIFFICULTY: Easy
PARKING: Park on either 68th St. or Fairview Ave., near Maxie's Restaurant
PUBLIC TRANSIT: MCTS route 76

Allowing for a few intrusions from the Village of Wauwatosa, this walk is otherwise entirely in the neighborhood of Bluemound Heights. Many Milwaukeeans reside here to enjoy the suburban feel of quiet streets while also remaining in the city.

According to Census Bureau data, Bluemound Heights consists of predominantly white, working-class families in health services and traditionally blue-collar jobs. Part of the neighborhood's feel comes from the presence of multiple trade union offices—especially in contrast with the two suburban neighborhoods on its northern border, which are even whiter and more affluent in terms of the residents' incomes and occupations.

Aside from statistics, let's get one thing clear: frozen custard is king in these parts. Frozen custard, a signature treat similar to ice cream but richer and creamier, is featured all across Milwaukee at myriad custard stands, but the oldest one, Gilles, is located in this West Side neighborhood.

The neighborhood is also home to other longstanding dining spots like Maxie's, a George Webb diner, Balistreri's Bluemound Inn, and Blue's Egg. That the regional headquarters of the Girl Scouts is here should also say something about Bluemound Heights.

Walk Description

Start near the intersection of North 68th Street and West Fairview Avenue. If the mouthwatering smells don't draw you over, the image of a fish wearing a crown on the front of the building should catch your eye. This is ❶ **Maxie's,** which serves Lowcountry Southern comfort food from the Carolinas, along with Creole and Cajun cuisine. Their jambalaya (called Jambalaya Me-Oh-My-A) is French Quarter worthy. Maxie's is also known for its barbecue and fresh seafood, including oysters and something called Frogmore Stew that you're just gonna have to stop in to find out about. The drink menu has all the Bourbon Street favorites, including Sazeracs, and mint juleps for the hat-and-horsey crowd on Derby Day. Maxie's is the place to be for Mardi Gras in Milwaukee with live, local brass bands and free-flowing Abita beers. *Laissez les bons temps rouler!*

Head north on 68th Street, with Maxie's to your right. Take a left on West Stevenson Street. To the right is the Marian Shrine, a quiet place for contemplation built by the Dominican Sisters in 1947. Continue west on Stevenson. This quiet street of mostly single-level homes is representative of the neighborhood. There are some larger apartment buildings six blocks west, across from Chinese Community Baptist Church.

Stevenson is interrupted at North 76th Street. Across the intersection is ❷ **Pius XI Catholic High School,** a private school with about 900 students. The school opened in 1930. The original building had four stories, and two more were added in 1957, making it the six-story facility it is today. Pius offers 200 courses, which is more than any other school in the state, and it has more national board-certified teachers than any other private school in Wisconsin. Pius XI has two team monikers: the Popes for the boys' teams and the Lady Popes for the girls' teams.

Turn right (north) on North 76th Street. On the right is ❸ **Brewski's Sports Club,** and as the name suggests it's a Milwaukee Brewers bar and restaurant. "Brewski" is also a nickname for beer, so that works too, considering they sell a lot of it here. (Remember, Milwaukee is Miller country!)

The walls are adorned with photos of great local athletes from the past, with a few photos of sports figures from opposing teams mixed in—those are hung upside down. Brewski's claims to be the home of the original Skittles shot, which is vodka infused with the colorful candy. The owner says other bars may claim to have invented the Skittles shot, but his version is one of a kind and features a secret infusing process that he's taking to his grave.

Across the street, ❹ Blue's Egg has taken Milwaukee by storm—and the long lines of customers waiting for breakfast and lunch prove it. Blue's Egg features a classic American diner menu with inspirations from around the world and Art Deco decor. Diners rave about the hash browns —specifically the Goat Cheese Browns that come with the Dubliner breakfast.

Turn right (east) on West Bluemound Road, which is also US 18 with the traffic to prove it. Behold the wonder of ❺ Gilles Frozen Custard, a fairly modest building but also the first custard stand in Milwaukee, founded in 1938. It's hard to understate the importance of custard in the city's identity. The rights to the Gilles Frozen Custard name were sold a long time ago, but there is no current affiliation between this Gilles and the Gilles brand sold in chain grocery stores throughout the United States, and Milwaukee's Gilles wants you to know that. As it reads on their website, "The bottom line is, if you buy it anyplace other than the Gilles Frozen Custard stand at 7515 West Bluemound Road you're not buying our custard." Gilles offers a flavor of the day, which is a popular concept in the world of custard. At the time of this writing, the flavor of the day was chocolate chip cookie dough.

Historical custard in hand, take a right out of the parking lot to continue east on Bluemound. The housing stock changes here to clapboard and brick two-story, single-family homes with the occasional stone Tudor in the mix. The suburb of Wauwatosa periodically dips down from the north for a few blocks, and then you're back in the city of Milwaukee. For those interested in knowing where they are at all times, look to the street signs at intersections: blue for Tosa, as Wauwatosa is often called, and green for Milwaukee. Where you see the occasional sign directing traffic to the Village of Wauwatosa, you might be inclined to ask, "Hey, aren't I already there?" But these signs are referring specifically to a commercial district along the Menomonee River.

Just past North 66th Street, about 10 blocks east of Gilles, is a notable place on the Tosa side of the line: ❻ Balistreri's Bluemound Inn, one of two restaurants owned by the Balistreri family, who have been in business four decades; the other restaurant, Balistreri's Italian/American Ristorante, is a couple of blocks north on 68th Street. The Bluemound Inn offers a lunch and dinner menu with dozens of gourmet pasta and ravioli plates, veal dishes, steaks, sandwiches, thin-crust pizzas, and Friday-only fish fries.

Balistreri's roughly begins a commercial stretch of automotive shops and parts stores, blue-collar bars, and union offices, including for the Communications Workers of America, the Wisconsin AFL-CIO, the AFL-CIO's Milwaukee Building and Construction Trades Council, and the Teamsters Local 200.

Just before North 59th Street, on the right, is **7** **McGinn's,** an Irish Brewers bar and restaurant with hundreds of bobbleheads on display. The lunch and dinner menus feature burgers, wings, Reubens, pork chops, ribs, steaks, salads, a Friday fish fry, and a lot of soup. The owner, Jeff Dobbe, has been a Brewers fan his entire life, but the one year he spent outside of Milwaukee, 1982, was the only year in Brewers history that the team made it to the World Series. Coincidence?

Kitty-corner is **8** **Barbiere's Italian Inn.** Sal Barbiere opened the restaurant in 1963 and moved the family business to its current location 10 years later. Barbiere retired in the late 1990s and sold the business to a longtime employee who also opened a second Italian comfort food restaurant in South Milwaukee in 2009.

Back across the street, next to another old-school sports bar, Steve's on Bluemound, sits **9** **Bark n' Scratch Outpost.** Its building a renovated automotive shop, Bark n' Scratch is a popular healthy pet food and supply store. One block up Bluemound is Calvary Cemetery and, just beyond, the beginning of the Story Hill walk (see page 176).

Turn right (south) on North Hawley Road. Halfway down the western edge of the cemetery, take a right (west) on West Park Hill Avenue, and then a quick left on North 59th Street. Follow 59th as it curves to the right, and then turn left on West Fairview Avenue—Fairview veers south before heading west again, but stay on course until 63rd Street. The I-94 freeway is a block to the left.

Turn right (north) on North 63rd Street at the **10** **Bluemound Heights Community Garden,** a green space behind Milwaukee Fire Station 35. The mix of frame housing welcomes you farther into this quiet neighborhood.

Take the next left onto West Mount Vernon Avenue. **11** **MacDowell Montessori School** is part of the Milwaukee Public Schools (MPS) system and offers education from kindergarten through high school. MPS has eight free Montessori schools in the district, including James Whitcomb Riley School, which is also bilingual.

Turn left (south) on 66th Street, along a tranquil tree-lined green space to the left and rows of bungalows to the right.

Turn right on Fairview Avenue to return to the start of the walk.

Bluemound Heights

Points of Interest

1. **Maxie's** 6732 W. Fairview Ave., 414-292-3969, maxies.com/milwaukee

2. **Pius XI Catholic High School** 135 N. 76th St., 414-290-7000, piusxi.org

3. **Blue's Egg** 317 N. 76th St., 414-299-3180, bluesegg.com

4. **Brewski's Sports Club** 304 N. 76th St., 414-475-0500

5. **Gilles Frozen Custard** 7515 W. Bluemound Road., 414-453-4875, gillesfrozencustard.com

6. **Balistreri's Bluemound Inn** 6501 W. Bluemound Road, 414-258-9881, balistreris.com

7. **McGinn's** 5901 W. Bluemound Road, 414-475-7546, mcginnsmilwaukee.com

8. **Barbiere's Italian Inn** 5844 W. Bluemound Road, 414-453-3800, barbieres.com

9. **Bark n' Scratch Outpost** 5835 W. Bluemound Road, 414-444-4110, milwaukeepetfood.com

10. **Bluemound Heights Community Garden** 6316 W. Fairview Ave.

11. **MacDowell Montessori School** 6415 W. Mount Vernon Ave., 414-935-1400, www5.milwaukee.k12.wi.us/school/macdowell

7 Bay View North
A Hot Spot with a History

Above: Hi-Fi Cafe, open since the mid-1990s, is one of Milwaukee's longest-running coffee shops.

BOUNDARIES: S. Hilbert St., E. Russell Ave., S. Lincoln Memorial Dr., S. Kinnickinnic Ave.
DISTANCE: Approximately 3 miles
DIFFICULTY: Easy
PARKING: On Kinnickinnic and Ward Sts.
PUBLIC TRANSIT: MCTS routes 15, 52, and Green Line

Trend-setting, community-focused Bay View is named for its proximity to and fabulous views of Lake Michigan's Milwaukee Bay. In 1879, Bay View became the first suburb of Milwaukee; prior to that, it was an independent village.

Since its inception, Bay View had a reputation of being a "company town" populated with diligent workers committed to their industrial employers, as well as to family and community.

During the late 19th and early 20th centuries, the neighborhood was home to the Milwaukee Iron Company, which primarily produced rails for railroads. Bay View became the epicenter for workers rights reform when industrial workers demanded a shortened, 8-hour workday. The resultant strike ended in the 1886 Bay View Massacre, in which the state militia gunned down seven mill workers, effectively ending the demonstrations but stirring up much more. Although the giant mills are long gone, Bay View remains home to numerous industrial sites, including Wrought Washer, Milwaukee Forge, and Klement's Sausage.

Most of Bay View's recent growth is rooted in hospitality and entertainment. On the north end of the neighborhood, mainstays like Groppi's Market and Club Garibaldi—businesses that inspired the area to once be known as Little Italy—continue to serve as anchors in the trendy lakeside scene. In the 1990s and 2000s, the neighborhood welcomed numerous new bars and restaurants, many of which are still thriving today.

Walk Description

Begin in ❶ **Zillman Park,** named after city alderman and newspaper publisher Erwin Zillman. On one end of the park is *Bud,* a steel tulip sculpture by Carl Billingsley, whose partner Catherine, a weaving artist, grew up in Bay View. Zillman was Catherine's grandfather. On the other end of the park is a historical marker commemorating Bay View's diverse immigrant community. Walk southeast on Kinnickinnic Avenue toward the marker and East Ward Street.

On the corner is ❷ **Cafe India,** serving authentic Indian cuisine with two locations in Milwaukee. Both have excellent lunch buffets, but this one is larger and has a full bar specializing in Indian beers and cocktails. The tandoori is particularly popular.

Across Ward Street, with a bright-green storefront, is ❸ **Bigfoot Bike and Skate,** an independently owned shop since 1985 and in its current space since 2011. In addition to stocking bikes, skateboards, roller skates, and scooters, the shop also participates in art events with exhibits of fine art–painted decks, and they are a sponsor of The Brewcity Bruisers, Milwaukee's women's Roller Derby team.

Continue southeast on South Kinnickinnic Avenue, or just KK to locals, along its densely packed commercial corridor. ❹ **Voyageur Book Shop,** on the left, is a used book shop that opened in 2017. The space is tidy and small with floor-to-ceiling bookshelves storing more than 12,000 books. There's also event and performance space on the lower level and a shop cat that roams freely.

Ahead on the right is the women-owned ❺ **Lulu Café & Bar** (some call it Cafe Lulu or just Lulu), a casual, upbeat bar and restaurant with excellent sandwiches, cocktails, and salads and one of the cutest signs in Milwaukee. It's also known for its homemade sides, like the Asian slaw and warm, homemade Lulu chips.

Across the street, ❻ **Stone Creek Coffee** is a chain of coffee shops that roast and serve their own. The shop is known for its commitment to fair relationships with farmers in Central and South America. They have 13 locations in Milwaukee, and they offer tours of their facilities.

Continuing southeast, at the next intersection is another cafe that's part of the local coffee chain ❼ **Colectivo.** This is followed by a long stretch of bars, including Tonic Tavern; restaurants, including Odd Duck and Café Corazón; a record shop; a longstanding comic book shop; and a locally beloved bowling alley, built in 1925. ❽ **Bay View Bowl** is a historic, 12-lane alley with a lively bar full of bowlers and nonbowlers alike. Bowling leagues remain very popular in Milwaukee, so bowling alleys have certain days and time frames reserved for league play.

On the right near the corner of East Homer Street is the recently restored ❾ **Avalon Atmospheric Theater,** known for its twinkly, starry ceiling and Spanish motif style. Built in 1929, the Avalon was open until 2000, when it closed, only to be reopened in 2014 after undergoing a $2 million revamp. Two theaters along with a bar and restaurant serve food and drink before, during, or after the films. Neighborhood Theater Group operates the Avalon as well as two other vintage theaters, Rosebud Cinema Drafthouse in Wauwatosa and The Times Cinema on the Vliet Street walk, page 126.

Continue southeast on KK as spaces become a little less packed together, passing newer condominiums and the Bay View branch of the Milwaukee Public Library. After a curve left and a gentle descent, note HI-FI Café, one of Milwaukee's longest-running coffee shops, on a prominent corner.

Turn left (east) on East Potter Avenue. Keep walking past ❿ **Burnhearts,** part of Bay View's new wave of businesses opened by millennials in the past 10–15 years. Burnhearts has an edgy-vintage feel with swag lamps hanging over the bar, sassy and kitschy-cute art hanging on the walls, and locally made Cedar Teeth frozen pizzas.

Here, Potter Avenue angles northeast; it's one of the many Bay View streets not adhering to any kind of modern planning grid. A couple more Milwaukee corner taverns line Potter in a largely residential section of the neighborhood that also includes ⓫ **T.H. Stemper Co.,** a religious goods and supplies store founded in 1911 and open to the public. It also has an impressive consignment room selling items from shuttered or demolished churches, including statues, pews, and altar candle stands.

Brinton Community Center is across from Stemper's with Beulah Brinton Park just beyond. Take a right (south) on South Bay Street and a left on East Russell Avenue. Cross under Lake Parkway/I-794.

12 **At Random** opened as a cocktail lounge in 1968 and, thanks to a dedicated new owner, continues to look and feel exactly the same as it did back in the day. Swag lamps, vinyl booths, electric fireplaces, and fancy cocktails—from spiked ice-cream beverages to a massive drink for two called the Tiki Love Bowl—are a few of the high points at this contemporary midcentury gem.

On the next block is **13** **G. Groppi Food Market,** a small Italian grocery store with a full deli, a butcher counter, and a bar. Giocondo and Giorgina Groppi founded the neighborhood staple in 1913. Grab some panini and cannoli to go, or stay for a cappuccino or a Bloody Mary—maybe even a cappuccino and a Bloody Mary.

Across the street on the next block you'll find **14** **Cactus Club,** a bar and live music venue that's been around for 20 years. Scads of local and national acts have played the back room, including The White Stripes, Queens of the Stone Age, Interpol, Death Cab for Cutie, Bright Eyes, Red Fang, and more.

Next door, **15** **Palomino Bar** is a classic Bay View spot serving drinks—including a large selection of whiskeys—and Southern-inspired comfort food like gumbo, po'boy sandwiches, brisket burgers, and chicken cracklings for dinner and brunch.

Across the street, **16** **Club Garibaldi** offers drinks, food, and live music in a space that has a large, dark wood bar with a tiny grill in one corner that somehow cranks out some of the city's best chicken wings. A marker across the street designates the site of the Bay View Massacre.

Russell Avenue curves left and goes downhill, becoming South Lincoln Memorial Drive, which will take you to the Port of Milwaukee and Jones Island. On your way down, note the U.S. Coast Guard station on the right and the dock for the Lake Express ferry behind it.

17 **Jones Island** is actually a peninsula that was once inhabited by a fishing community of predominantly immigrant Kashubes, an ethnic minority from the north of Poland. Today, it is known for its massive piles of road salt, offloaded from ships that travel the Great Lakes and beyond; the port where they dock; and the distinct, sometimes unpleasant odor from a Milwaukee-made fertilizer called Milorganite.

Turn left on East Lincoln Avenue, which climbs above the freeway and the "island." Bay View is a dog-friendly neighborhood, so the small dog park below the Lincoln Avenue bridge is a popular spot, particularly on weekends and after work. This is one of seven dog parks run by Milwaukee County.

Lincoln descends to East Bay Street. Follow the multiple curves of Bay along a line of large, now mostly to periodically empty industrial sites, but also the 225,000-square-foot factory

Locally owned Enlightened Brewing Company has as many as 12 beers on tap at any given time.

headquarters of **18** **Wrought Washer Manufacturing** (washers as in what goes around a bolt, not a washing machine), which has additional factories across the country and claims to be the world's largest washer manufacturer.

In 0.4 mile, hang a right on South Allis Street and head toward **19** **Enlightened Brewing Company.** The locally owned 10-barrel brewhouse produces roughly 3,000 barrels of beer annually. Their signature brews include a cream ale called Cream City Brix—named after the light-colored bricks that are Milwaukee's most prominent building material.

Take a right on East Stewart Street and a left on South Marine Drive. Walk across railroad tracks and next to a large parking lot to a boat-storage warehouse. With a gate blocking a private access road ahead of you, take a left in front of the warehouse. On the left are open-air boat storage and more warehouses; to the right, a long fence and the Kinnickinnic River just beyond.

On your right, beyond a fence and a warehouse for boat storage company Skipper Bud's, is **⑳ Barnacle Bud's,** a well-hidden bar/restaurant with a massive patio and boat slips on the edge of the Kinnickinnic River. Bud's is one of Milwaukee's most beloved hidden gems and is often described by locals as having a Florida feel. Prior to readily available GPS and smartphones, the lively summer oasis was sometimes impossible for seekers to find, which made it even more alluring to locals and visitors alike.

Continue south on South Hilbert Street, a winding lane that at times will seem like an alley, past more warehouses, silos, and the train tracks again.

Eventually, on your left **㉑ Santino's Little Italy** appears. Opened in 2017 but with a truly old-school vibe, the cozy and artistic eatery offers a variety of Italian food. The notable decor includes a red abstract painting on the ceiling done by a Bay View artist and a painted sign on one of the doors that's a nod to the film *The Godfather*. Can you find it?

Continue south on Hilbert back to East Bay Street and take a right, then a left to navigate some traffic turn lanes, and a final left on Kinnickinnic. Zillman Park is again ahead on your left.

Points of Interest

① **Zillman Park** 2168 S. Kinnickinnic Ave.

② **Cafe India** 2201 S. Kinnickinnic Ave., 414-837-6121, cafeindiamke.us

③ **Bigfoot Bike and Skate** 350 E. Ward St., 414-332-3479, bigfootbikeandskate.com

④ **Voyager Book Shop** 2212 S. Kinnickinnic Ave., 414-210-3309, voyageurbookshop.com

⑤ **Lulu Café & Bar** 2261 S. Howell Ave., 414-294-5858, lulubayview.com

⑥ **Stone Creek Coffee** 2266 S. Kinnickinnic Ave., 414-481-4215, stonecreekcoffee.com

⑦ **Colectivo–Bay View** 2301 S. Kinnickinnic Ave., 414-744-6117, colectivocoffee.com

⑧ **Bay View Bowl** 2416 S. Kinnickinnic Ave., 414-483-0950, bayviewbowlwi.com

⑨ **Avalon Atmospheric Theater** 2473 S. Kinnickinnic Ave., 414-539-6678, avalonmke.com

⑩ **Burnhearts** 2599 S. Logan Ave., 414-294-0490, burnheartsbar.com

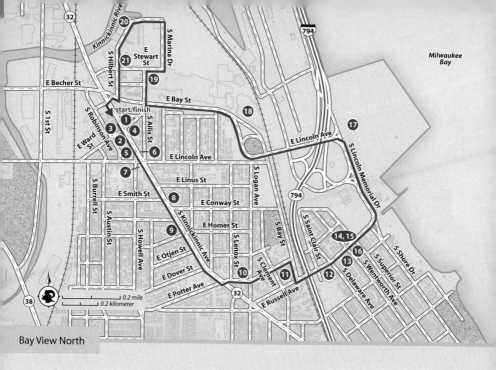

11 T.H. Stemper Co. 1125 E. Potter Ave., 414-744-3610, stempers.com

12 At Random 2501 S. Delaware Ave., 414-481-8030, atrandommke.com

13 G. Groppi Food Market 1441 E. Russell Ave., 414-747-9012, facebook.com/GroppisMarket

14 Cactus Club 2496 S. Wentworth Ave., 414-897-0663, cactusclubmilwaukee.com

15 Palomino Bar 2491 S. Superior St., 414-747-1007, palominobar.com

16 Club Garibaldi 2501 S. Superior St., 414-483-6335, clubgaribaldi.com

17 Jones Island mmsd.com/what-we-do/wastewater-treatment

18 Wrought Washer Manufacturing 2100 S. Bay St., 800-558-5217, wroughtwasher.com

19 Enlightened Brewing Company 2020 S. Allis St., 414-704-4085, enlightenedbeer.com

20 Barnacle Bud's 1955 S. Hilbert St., 414-481-9974, barnaclebuds.com

21 Santino's Little Italy 352 E. Stewart St., 414-897-7367, santinoslittleitaly.com

8 Bay View South
Beautiful Parks in a Strong Community

Above: Stop at Krieg's Lakeside Bakery (formerly Canfora Bakery) for pączki, a Milwaukee tradition.

BOUNDARIES: E. Pryor Ave., E. Oklahoma Ave., S. Shore Dr., Park Rd.
DISTANCE: Approximately 4 miles
DIFFICULTY: Easy
PARKING: Park on the street along Delaware or New York Aves.
PUBLIC TRANSIT: MCTS route 51

Historically, Bay View was known for its blue-collar workers and strong community. This largely remains true of the area in general, along with nearby neighborhoods Fernwood, Tippecanoe, and the Town of Lake, all just south of this walk. But since the 1990s, Bay View has also attracted many artists and young entrepreneurs who have created a trendy new dimension to the neighborhood, particularly on its north end. The southern end of the neighborhood, experienced on this walk, is quieter and more residential, but here too the infusion of new culture is felt, putting Bay View on the Milwaukee map as one of the best neighborhoods to live, socialize, and—because of its proximity to Lake Michigan—experience nature.

Walk Description

Begin at South Delaware Avenue and East Oklahoma Avenue, in a small commercial district in an otherwise quiet part of Bay View. Walk east toward Lake Michigan on Oklahoma to its beginning at South Superior Street. Across the intersection is a trailhead for the Oak Leaf Trail in ❶ **Bay View Park,** a 40-acre beauty in the county park system that hugs the lakeshore to the south.

Take a left on Superior Street to walk by bungalows of various styles, including Arts and Crafts, and various facades—stucco, brick, and stone—mixed in with more stately homes; all of the houses to your right on this first block belie deep backyards to the lake bluff.

Turn right on Texas Avenue, which opens up a wide lake view. Follow the sidewalk to South Shore Drive, and take a left. This appropriately named street follows the shore northwest along a marina to South Shore Park and its ❷ **South Shore Terrace Kitchen + Beer Garden.** This former 1930s bathhouse is now the home of the Miller 1855 beer garden with nice views of the lake and a nearby pier to walk out on. The Terrace is a Milwaukee county park, so food and drink profits funnel back into the community. It was largely funded by Molson Coors; thus there are roughly 12 Molson Coors options, from Miller Lite to Blue Moon. Wine, hard cider, soda (yes, we say soda in Milwaukee, as opposed to pop), and water are also available. Dogs and kids are welcome and abundant here, creating a family-friendly vibe.

Bringing children to beer gardens is socially acceptable in Milwaukee—as it is in other cities—but Milwaukee has a long, controversial yet legal history of kids "growing up" in bars and taverns. Parents were more likely to bring their kids regularly into bars in the '70s, '80s, and '90s, but it is still part of Milwaukee culture today and a topic on which natives have very mixed opinions. In general, drinking culture is complicated in Brew City.

Take a right (northeast) on Nock Street. ❸ **The South Shore Yacht Club** started in 1913 and today prides itself on its affordability, lack of pretension, and ability to serve as a fun entertainment outlet year-round. The club has hosted the Queen's Cup Race across Lake Michigan since 1938, which makes the competition even older than the America's Cup. To the northwest, tiny ❹ **Cupertino Park** is only 7 acres but features community gardens, a pier, and a water utility building. It was once part of South Shore Park but in 1997 separated in order to honor former park commissioner and county supervisor Daniel Cupertino.

Take a left (northwest) on East Iron Street, which is indistinguishable from the yacht club's parking lot at this point, and then follow it as it curves left away from the lake. At the top of the hill, take a right (northwest) on South Superior Street. ❺ **The Beulah Brinton House** is the headquarters for the Bay View Historical Society and named for a respected resident of the neighborhood. In the 1870s, immigrants moved to Bay View to work at the Bay View Rolling Mill, and Brinton welcomed many into her home, where she taught them reading in English, sewing, and other skills. Today the space is also used for community meetings, small performances, and events. The Little Free Library in front of the Beulah Brinton House is often worth browsing.

Take a left (southwest) on East Pryor Avenue. The ❻ **Pryor Avenue Iron Well** was built in 1882 and named for its iron-rich water. Originally it was drilled to provide drinking water and fire protection. According to the Milwaukee Historic Preservation Committee, it is the last public well in Milwaukee and was named a historic structure in 1987. Despite its proximity to Lake Michigan, its source of water is actually an underground layer of rock, called an aquifer, that is located 118 feet below the surface. Although the well is still accessed today by many for fresh drinking water, it has an acquired taste. Some people think the water tastes like pennies; others say it tastes like blood. We think it tastes cool and refreshing . . . and a little like pennies.

Continue on Pryor Avenue. The Lewis Fieldhouse will be on your right as you walk under the Lake Parkway freeway bridge. Turn left (south) on California Street and cross busy Kinnickinnic Avenue. ❼ **Classic Slice,** which opened in 2007 and features the Milwaukee-famous Illuminati/pizza-slice logo, is one of Milwaukee's iconic pizza joints known for its bountiful selection of toppings—from vegan to bacon—and fun, casual neighborhood vibe. Classic Slice also serves tasty calzones, salads, and ciabatta sandwiches.

Continue south on California. Kinnickinnic Park will be on your left. Take a right (west) on East Manitoba Street. ❽ **Tenuta's Italian Restaurant** was founded in 2003 by a couple who moved to Milwaukee from the southern tip of Italy. Over the years, it has been consistently voted a favorite spot for Italian cuisine by readers and editors of numerous Milwaukee publications; it was voted Best Italian Restaurant by *OnMilwaukee* in 2018. Authentic and quaint, the restaurant's decor is modern-meets-1940s. The menu features all the Italian classics: homemade pizza and ravioli, salads, pastas, and a standout tiramisu. The lasagna is pretty incredible too. In 2019 Tenuta's opened a to-go version of the restaurant, also in the Bay View neighborhood.

Take a right (north) on South Logan Avenue as Manitoba ends at ❾ **Humboldt Park.** Hilly Humboldt Park was one of the first six parks created in Milwaukee when the city started a park commission in 1890. It features 73 acres of beautiful scenery, including trails, ponds, cultural events, a beer and wine garden, and many other amenities. An outdoor music stage hosts weekly, family-friendly Tuesday night concerts in the summer, called Chill on the Hill, as well as many other music events and festivals, including the Puerto Rican Festival, WMSE Backyard BBQ, and Global Union Festival.

A wintry pier on icy Lake Michigan

Turn left (west) on East Idaho Street, with the park to your left and, ahead, the Humboldt Park pond. Take a left (south) on Park Road, the pond to your left now, and ⑩ **The Vine Humboldt Wine & Beer Garden** on your right. Open only in the summer, The Vine serves five wines on tap, craft beer, and Peruvian empanadas. Beverages purchased at The Vine can be carried throughout the park, and proceeds support future park projects. Like the South Shore Terrace, The Vine is dog and kid friendly.

Follow the road out of the park to take a left (east) on East Oklahoma Avenue. Three blocks down on the left is ⑪ **Krieg's Lakeside Bakery** (formerly Canfora Bakery), locally famous for its hot ham and rolls (a Sunday tradition in Milwaukee); Italian cookies; and pączki (pronounced pawnch-key), Polish donuts filled with jelly or creme that are sold primarily at the beginning of Lent. *OnMilwaukee* food writer Lori Fredrich writes, "It's important to note that pączki aren't just jelly-filled doughnuts. In fact, what sets them apart is their dough, which is a rich, sweet yeast dough consisting of eggs, butter, and milk." Indeed, Fat Tuesday—which started as a time to use up fats and eggs before the Lenten fast—is known as Pączki Day in Milwaukee. Today, many Milwaukee office kitchens are well stocked with pączki on this "everyone's Polish on Pączki Day" holiday.

In four blocks you reach the Lake Parkway freeway bridge again. On the left is ⑫ **Milwaukee Forge,** creator of gears, shafts, nuts, valves, flanges, bearings, ground-engaging tools, and other forged items ranging from 2 to 100 pounds. Milwaukee Forge opened in 1913 and has been at its current location since 1918. Today the $35 million company employees 125 workers.

Continue east on Oklahoma, crossing Kinnickinnic Avenue again. It's still a commercial corridor, but businesses aren't as densely packed together here as on Kinnickinnic's north end, in the Bay View North walk (page 37).

Continue three more blocks to return to the beginning of the walk.

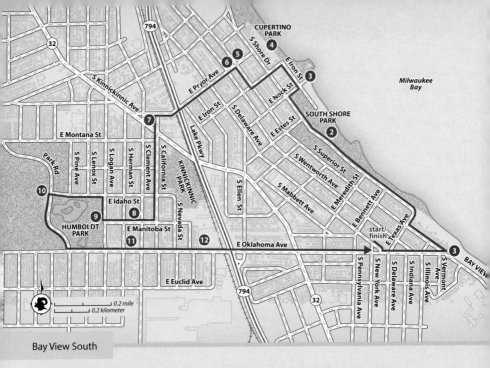

Points of Interest

1. **Bay View Park** 3120 S. Lake Drive, 414-257-7275, countyparks.com

2. **South Shore Terrace Kitchen + Beer Garden** 2900 S. Shore Dr., 414-257-7275, southshoreterrace.com

3. **South Shore Yacht Club** 2300 E. Nock St., 414-481-2331, ssyc.org

4. **Cupertino Park** 2000 E. Iron St., 414-257-7275, countyparks.com

5. **Beulah Brinton House** 2590 S. Superior St., 414-273-8288, bayviewhistoricalsociety.org

6. **Pryor Avenue Iron Well** tinyurl.com/pryoraveironwell

7. **Classic Slice** 2797 S. Kinnickinnic Ave., 414-238-2406, classicslice.com

8. **Tenuta's Italian Restaurant** 2995 S. Clement Ave., 414-431-1014, tenutasitalian.com

9. **Humboldt Park** 3000 S. Howell Ave., 414-257-7275, countyparks.com

10. **The Vine Humboldt Wine & Beer Garden** 3000 S. Howell Ave., 414-257-7275, humboldtparkmilwaukee.org/park-amenities/humboldt-park-beer-garden

11. **Krieg's Lakeside Bakery** 1100 E. Oklahoma Ave., 414-486-7747, canforabakeryinc.com

12. **Milwaukee Forge** 1532 E. Oklahoma Ave., 414-744-4565, milwaukeeforge.com

9 Pigsville
Come for the Bacon, Stay for the Beer

Above: The historic Valley Inn, a tavern and town meeting place since 1905

BOUNDARIES: W. Michigan St., W. Mount Vernon Ave., N. 35th St., N. 42nd St.
DISTANCE: Approximately 1.5 miles
DIFFICULTY: Moderate (for going up and down the old river bluffs)
PARKING: Free street parking at N. 42nd St. and W. Saint Paul Ave.
PUBLIC TRANSIT: MCTS routes 35 (N. 35th St.) and Gold Line (W. Wisconsin Ave., north of the walk)

The secluded Pigsville neighborhood—also called Piggsville, Valley Park, or just The Valley—is practically hidden because it's located below the Wisconsin Avenue viaduct and bounded by steep river bluffs. It's also the only residential area in the otherwise industrial Menomonee Valley.

No one is certain, but the neighborhood's quirky name may be from a large pig farm that was located near here in the late 19th century, or from a man named George Pigg, but this is disputed. At any rate, the area was settled, in general, mostly by German Lutheran immigrant farmers who were later joined by Eastern Europeans, notably Slovaks.

Pigsville is primarily a residential area of wood-frame houses and bungalows built in the early 20th century. Due to its isolation from the rest of the city, Pigsville has always been a close-knit community. Because it's situated in a valley, flooding is common and flood damage has been an unfortunate downside to living here.

Miller Brewery is visible from many parts of the neighborhood, and its beer flows plentifully at Pigsville's historic Valley Inn.

Walk Description

Park at North 42nd Street and West Saint Paul Avenue on the dead-end street bordering Valley Park. To the north, the Miller Brewery sign is visible in the distance; to the south, catch a glimpse of American Family Field, formerly Miller Park, the home of the Milwaukee Brewers.

Head into ❶ Valley Park on any of the many footpaths along South 42nd Street, and check out the Menomonee River, as well as the war memorial erected in 1948 to commemorate the neighborhood's World War II dead. In the late 1990s, after two back-to-back "100-year storms," the new river wall, replacing a Works Progress Administration–era floodwall, was finally constructed to stem the persistent flooding that plagued the neighborhood's entire history. At the time, 18 homes were removed as well, reducing the number of houses in the area to around 100.

Winter in Valley Park, located beside the Menomonee River

Hardships aside, residents have strong Pigsville pride, and many families have remained in the area for generations. The tight-knit community has a good sense of humor about the name too. Once, during a talk about 19th-century Pigsville by Milwaukee historian John Gurda, many of the audience members showed up wearing pig noses. During the talk, Gurda called the neighborhood "the most unusual place name in Milwaukee."

In the park, there's a nice contrast between the sound of the water to the west, the traffic on I-94 to the south, the Miller Brewing truck lot up the hill to the north, and virtually no sound from the secluded working-class neighborhood of modest but well-kept homes.

Neighbors work together to keep the park—and the neighborhood—safe and clean via the Friends of Valley Park & Gardens neighborhood group and an active Facebook page notifying folks of frequent community events, including Valley Park Beauty Day, bonfires, a garden crawl, and plant and seed exchanges.

Head south out of the park and left onto West Mount Vernon Avenue. Go east two short blocks, then take a left on North 41st Street. Head up the long block and hang a right on West Saint Paul Avenue.

Walk east four blocks, with the homes mostly facing the cross streets, and then West Saint Paul Avenue gets a little curvy as it winds its way up the old river bluff. Crossing North 39th Street, successful hill climbers will have officially left Pigsville and entered the adjacent Merrill Park neighborhood. On the left is ❷ **Quad Park,** an athletic field for the Marquette University High School Hilltoppers. The school itself is to the north farther along on the walk.

The Merrill Park neighborhood extends east to North 27th Street. After railroad manager Sherburn Merrill founded the new development in 1883, many of its earliest residents were Milwaukee Irish displaced by the Third Ward Fire of 1892. Among the notable Merrill Park residents was Oscar-winning actor Spencer Tracy, who was born on North 30th Street in 1900.

Take a left (north) on North 35th Street and walk along ❸ **Merrill Park,** which since its founding has served as a major meeting place for neighborhood residents. Across North 35th Street to the northeast is ❹ **Marquette University High School** (MUHS) a private, all-male Jesuit institution dating back to 1857 in downtown Milwaukee. The school moved to its current location in 1922. Marquette teams have won 28 Wisconsin Interscholastic Athletic Association (WIAA) state titles in soccer, volleyball, tennis, baseball, and football. Milwaukee mayor Tom Barrett graduated from MUHS, as did that neighborhood kid Spencer Tracy.

The school's Quad Park athletic field was named in part after a donor, the late Betty Quadracci, longtime publisher of *Milwaukee Magazine.* In 1971, Betty and her husband, Harry V. Quadracci,

Pigsville is primarily a working-class neighborhood.

launched Quad/Graphics, one of the world's leading printing companies. Over the years, she donated millions of dollars to the Milwaukee Art Museum, among other interests. She died in 2013.

At West Michigan Street, hang a left and continue walking the contours of the park; take another left on North 36th Street and immediately turn right, back onto West Michigan Street. Follow West Michigan Street a couple of blocks back down the bluff and again into Pigsville, taking a left (south) on North 39th Street.

At West Clybourn Street, take a right. A couple of short blocks ahead of you on the right is the ❺ Valley Inn—and just in time, as we're certain all this walking has worked up a proper Milwaukee thirst. If not, Valley Inn is still worth a stop for lunch. Ask for the Pig Sandwich—it's not on the menu, but it's the house specialty. James Hutterer, the current owner, who was born in the apartment above the tavern, still works behind the bar sometimes. The Valley Inn has been in the same family since the early 1960s. Hutterer, who took over the business in 1996, has many memories of the bar as a child. He recalls a fire breaking out in 1963 while his father was burning boxes in the basement incinerator, and his mom wouldn't let 4-year-old James go into the basement to "save" his dad. Luckily, his father made it out safely and there was only minimal damage to the building.

Built in 1898, the Valley Inn has been a tavern since at least 1905. The well-liked and long-standing, if the only, gathering place for the neighborhood, it is also a popular destination before

and after Brewers games. It has also been an unofficial bar for many folks who work up the valley for Molson Coors.

If you ever feel like leaving Valley Inn, and we wouldn't blame you if you don't, take a right once you're out the door. The river is visible again two blocks up the street. Take another glimpse, but sometimes what is essentially an alley up ahead is not navigable, so take a left instead a couple of blocks on, at North 41st Street, and then a right on West Saint Paul Avenue to return to Valley Park.

Points of Interest

1 **Valley Park** 343 N. 42nd St, 414-257-7275, countyparks.com

2 **Quad Park** 3800 W. Saint Paul Ave.

3 **Merrill Park** 461 N. 35th St.

4 **Marquette University High School** 3401 W. Wisconsin Ave., 414-933-7220, muhs.edu

5 **Valley Inn** 400 W. Clybourn St., 414-344-1158

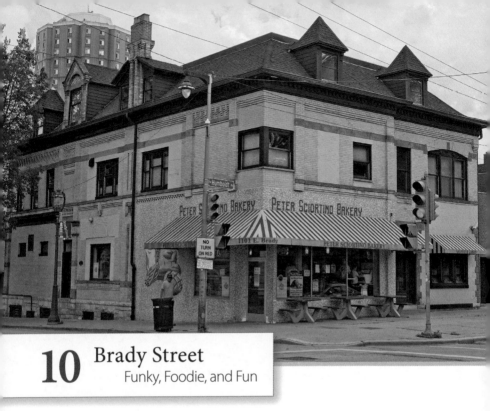

10 Brady Street
Funky, Foodie, and Fun

Above: Peter Sciortino Bakery is known for its from-scratch pastries, made daily.

BOUNDARIES: N. Commerce St., E. Brady St., N. Warren Ave., Marsupial Bridge/N. Holton St.
DISTANCE: Approximately 2 miles
DIFFICULTY: Easy
PARKING: Free street parking just north of Brady Street near Swing Park
PUBLIC TRANSIT: MCTS routes 15 (Holton) and Green Line (Brady)

Inhabited by Irish, German, and Italian immigrants in the 1860s and repopulated by the hippies 100 years later, the modern Brady Street area encompasses the best of the old and the new.

This fun part of town stretches between Lake Michigan and the Milwaukee River and has a trendy and eclectic—now slightly upscale—vibe. It's packed with old-school and contemporary restaurants, specialty retail shops, ethnic cuisine, coffee shops, tattoo shops, salons, and a vibrant nightlife.

Residents of the neighborhood are as diverse as the structures they live in, which include high-rise towers on Prospect, Victorian beauties just south of Brady Street, and apartment complexes rented primarily by students and younger folk.

Brady Street has been and likely always will be one of Milwaukee's most beloved destinations.

Walk Description

Begin at ❶ **Swing Park,** which is underneath the Holton Street viaduct off North Water Street and across from East Pearson Street. The park's swings—made from recycled materials—dangle from the bottom of the bridge. Initially a project of University of Wisconsin–Milwaukee urban planning graduate students and community activists, the park earned its official status with a ribbon cutting from the city in 2014 and is now host to bike-in movies and many other small-scale, community-oriented events.

From the park, walk the Marsupial Bridge, which spans the Milwaukee River suspended from the Holton Street bridge above. Enjoy the views above the water along an increasingly green stretch of renewed waterway lined with newer condos and restaurants where some of the city's many tanneries once lined the banks and polluted the water in a bustling industrial corridor.

On the other side of the bridge is ❷ **Lakefront Brewery.** In 1987, two brothers and a friend started brewing beer in a former bakery in the Riverwest neighborhood. They sold the first barrel of their now-flagship beer, Riverwest Stein, to a neighborhood watering hole called Gordon Park Pub. Today, Lakefront Brewery produces about 50,000 barrels a year in this much larger facility that once housed the Milwaukee Electric Railway and Light Company's coal-fired power plant. Lakefront's award-winning tour is one of the best in the city—and includes four glasses of beer! There's also a restaurant called Beer Hall inside the building that serves sausage flights and a fish fry, and on Fridays they host a live polka band called the Brewhaus Polka Kings.

Take the stairs or the pedestrian path (a continuation of the Oak Leaf Trail, of which the Marsupial is also a part) down to North Commerce Street, and head northeast (left, if you are facing Commerce Street at the bottom of the stairs).

After 0.25 mile, hang a right on North Riverboat Road, which angles down toward the river and underneath the North Humboldt Avenue bridge, past ❸ **The Beerline Cafe,** one of Milwaukee's few all-vegetarian eateries (it also offers vegan items). Healthy-food restaurants and Milwaukee have not always gone hand in hand. For a long time, Milwaukee was known for heavy German restaurants, burger joints, diners, and basically cheese melted over everything. In recent

Soccer fans gather to watch games at Nomad World Pub, one of two fútbol bars in the city.

years, however, the city has welcomed more and more health-conscious restaurants, both chains and locally owned. We still like melted cheese an awful lot, though.

Take a right and walk up the steep but short road to the Humboldt Avenue bridge alongside more newer construction and ❹ **Stubby's Gastrogrub & Beer Bar,** a bar with a large patio overlooking the river. Before you start the incline, cast one more glance down Riverboat Road toward a curve that masks a hidden gem. The road dead-ends at the Beerline Trail and crosses the river where the much maligned North Avenue Dam once stood to Caesar's Park, a quiet stretch of riverfront below public housing at the north end of the Brady Street neighborhood.

But you're on this walk to check out some of the oldest working-class housing and hangouts in the city, so head south on Humboldt Avenue back across the river, where you'll find a couple of restaurants, including ❺ **BelAir Cantina,** a local chain of Mexican-fusion restaurants serving mix-and-match street tacos, and a lounge called Fink's.

Take a left on East Kane Place and a fairly quick right on North Pulaski Street. The winding street leads past the 110-year-old ❻ **Wolski's Tavern,** one of Milwaukee's most famous watering holes. They give away free I CLOSED WOLSKI'S bumper stickers to wee-hours-of-the-morning drinkers (closing time is 2 a.m. during the week and 2:30 a.m. on weekends). The stickers have been spotted and photographed all over the world.

Beyond a somewhat odd bend in this old and narrow city street sits Peters-Weiland & Co. pipe organ tuning and repair shop. Built in 1918, it's one of the last of its kind in the country. (Milwaukee is also home to one of the last "pipe organ pizza" joints in the country, called Organ Piper Pizza.)

At the end of Pulaski, you'll find ❼ **Thurman's 15,** a staple and eclectic East Side tavern that's part sports bar, part Grateful Dead/Phish tribute bar, and part classic corner tap.

Take a left on North Arlington Place. Those who dig midcentury lounges and kitschy art should take note of ❽ **Jamo's**—where there's a bizarre painting of Jesus blessing the United Nations—a block north on the corner of East Hamilton Street, where you'll take a right. Take another right on North Warren Avenue, which will put you back on Brady Street across from ❾ **Nomad World Pub,** one of Milwaukee's two soccer (*fútbol*) bars (this one also has a second location in Madison, Wisconsin). Along with the equally iconic Hi Hat down the street, Nomad was at the forefront of the Brady Street revival in the post-hippie urban renewal of the mid-'90s.

Go right (west) to the ❿ **Hi Hat & Garage on Brady,** on the right. The Hi Hat lounge introduced the concept of craft cocktails to the East Side in 1998 and never stopped mixing 'em. It also has a full menu and a popular brunch. The attached, more casual restaurant is called the Garage.

Opposite Hi Hat is ⓫ **Rochambo** coffee and tea house, a Milwaukee staple serving Valentine coffee (which also makes a killer Irish coffee), craft beer, upscale spirits, and more than 40 teas, in the middle of a densely lined block.

Continue west along Brady Street. Italian culture runs throughout this historic yet trendy neighborhood. The iconic ⓬ **Peter Sciortino Bakery** is known for its breads, cookies, and Italian pastries (ask a native if they know who's locally famous for chanting, "Pepperoni! Cannoli!").

Before taking a right (north) at Saint Hedwig's church on North Humboldt Avenue, glance over to the opposite corner at ⓭ **Art Smart's Dart Mart & Juggling Emporium.** This business has occupied its corner spot since the 1970s.

Wolski's Tavern has been in operation for more than a century.

Whereas it once specialized in darts and juggling supplies, today it also stocks a solid selection of disc golf gear, novelty items, and silly gifts, from whoopee cushions and unique adhesive bandages to pickle-flavored candy.

Two blocks north on Humboldt is **⑭ Pitch's Lounge & Restaurant,** an old-school supper club–meets–classic Milwaukee tavern with heaping plates of barbecue ribs atop tables with white tablecloths. Pitch's opened in 1942 and is currently run by the owner's son. Get the spumoni for dessert.

On the next block, **⑮ Scaffidi's Hideout,** popular for billiards as well as its Lower East Side feel, has been in operation for nearly 40 years in a building that has housed taverns since at least 1891.

Take a left on East Land Place and another left on North Astor Street. Soak up this relatively quiet part of the neighborhood on the way back to Brady, where the **⑯ Emperor of China** awaits you on the corner. This classic Chinese restaurant has been around since 1986, an eternity for most restaurants on a trendy block.

Across Brady stands another longtime business, **⑰ Glorioso's Italian Market,** a grocery store, wine shop, deli, bakery, and café that's been in operation for almost 75 years. Across the street (its original location), Glorioso's also has a space with a kitchen where it now offers cooking classes and special events.

Turn right (west) on Brady. At the intersection with North Cass Street is **⑱ Casablanca,** a double-decker Middle Eastern restaurant. The interior is just as grand as the exterior with chandeliers, a beautiful staircase, richly painted walls, and lush plants. Hookah service is available in the bar, and the weekday lunch buffet is completely vegetarian. (Casablanca has meat dishes on the regular menu.)

If you're returning to the starting point, take a right on North Cass Street and then a left on East Pearson Street, where your seat at Swing Park will still be warm. Public transit riders will find their stops at the intersection of East Brady and North Holton Streets one block straight ahead.

Points of Interest

① Swing Park 1737 N. Water St.

② Lakefront Brewery 1872 N. Commerce St., 414-372-8800, lakefrontbrewery.com

③ Beerline Cafe 2076 N. Commerce St., 414-265-5644, beerlinecafe.com

④ Stubby's Gastrogrub & Beer Bar 2060 N. Humboldt Ave., 414-763-6324, stubbysgastrogrub.com

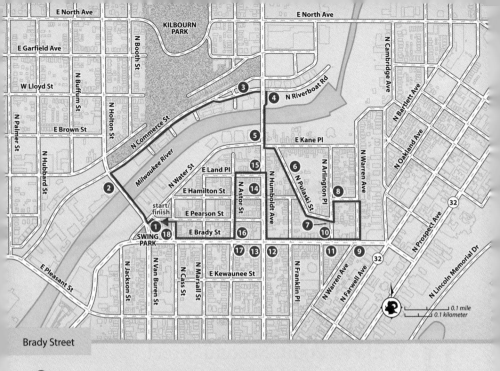

Brady Street

⑤ **BelAir Cantina** 1935 N. Water St., 414-226-2245, belaircantina.com

⑥ **Wolski's Tavern** 1836 N. Pulaski St., 414-276-8130, wolskis.com

⑦ **Thurman's 15** 1731 N. Arlington Place, 414-224-1080

⑧ **Jamo's** 1800 N. Arlington Place, 414-276-7101

⑨ **Nomad World Pub** 1401 E. Brady St., 414-224-8111, nomadworldpub.com

⑩ **Hi Hat & Garage on Brady** 1701 N. Arlington Place, 414-225-9330, hihatlounge.com

⑪ **Rochambo** 1317 E. Brady St., 414-291-0095, rochambo.com

⑫ **Peter Sciortino Bakery** 1101 E. Brady St., 414-272-4623, petersciortinosbakery.com

⑬ **Art Smart's Dart Mart & Juggling Emporium** 1695 N. Humboldt Ave., 414-273-3278, jugglingsupplies.net

⑭ **Pitch's Lounge & Restaurant** 1801 N. Humboldt Ave., 414-272-9313, pitchsribs.com

⑮ **Scaffidi's Hideout** 1837 N. Humboldt Ave., 414-273-1665, scaffidishideout.com

⑯ **Emperor of China** 1010 E. Brady St., 414-271-8889, emperorofchinarestaurant.com

⑰ **Glorioso's Italian Market** 1011 E. Brady St., 414-272-0540, gloriosos.com

⑱ **Casablanca** 728 E. Brady St., 414-271-6000, casablancaonbrady.com

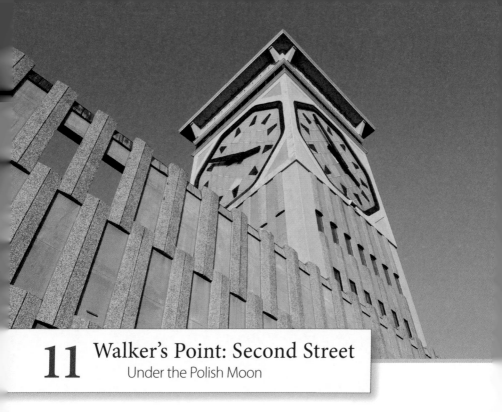

11 Walker's Point: Second Street
Under the Polish Moon

Above: The Allen-Bradley Clock, aka the Polish Moon, is the world's second-largest four-sided clock.

BOUNDARIES: Menomonee River, Scott St., S. Water St., S. Second St.
DISTANCE: Approximately 2.5 miles
DIFFICULTY: Easy
PARKING: Street parking on north end of S. Second St. between the Menomonee River and Freshwater Way
PUBLIC TRANSIT: Bus routes 19, 23, and 15 (1 block east); The Hop streetcar: Saint Paul at Plankinton stop (2 blocks north)

Once a rice marsh turned fur-trading site, Walker's Point is the oldest neighborhood in Milwaukee and today offers some of the city's most innovative restaurants, bars, shops, and art galleries alongside some of its oldest homes—and sometimes in them. The area has a number of LGBTQ bars, eateries, and nightclubs and is aptly nicknamed The Gayborhood. Walker's Point is also known for its vibrant Latin community that has contributed dozens of delicious local Mexican restaurants that are visited by Milwaukeeans from neighborhoods near and far.

Although Walker's Point technically stretches west to 14th Street, most of the action takes place on South Second Street—although recently South Fifth Street has become a neighborhood hot spot as well (see Walk 12, page 66). Within a mile, there are brunch, lunch, dinner, and late-night eats available, all of which are stumbling distance from a corner tap, craft cocktail lounge, lesbian sports tavern, motorcycle bar, and more.

Second Street has served as the route for the Pride Parade for more than a decade, and during the entire month of June the street is lined with rainbow flags.

Walk Description

Start on South Second Street near the Menomonee River adjacent a sprawling row of 19th-century warehouses. One of these on the east side of South Second is the block-long 1892 ❶ **Lindsay Building.** The Cream City brick exterior constructed around massive oak columns (think: entire trees) formerly housed everything from buggies and sleighs to agricultural equipment. It's occasionally used for special events.

Walk south on South Second Street, away from the river. At Freshwater Way/Pittsburgh Avenue, note ❷ **Purple Door Ice Cream,** a brave local business serving innovative, artisan ice cream in a city where frozen custard is king. There are now three Purple Door locations, including one that's on the Sherman Park walk (page 131), but this is the original. Stop in and try the Old Fashioned ice cream in honor of Wisconsin's favorite cocktail (made with brandy, not whiskey, in these parts).

Continue walking toward the large, white-faced clock that towers over the middle of the street in the distance. Once the largest four-sided clock in the world, it is officially called the Allen-Bradley Clock but is also known to locals as the Polish Moon in honor of the once-dense Polish population in the area.

❸ **Caroline's** offers live jazz and blues on a small stage for intimate shows most nights of the week. The 365-degree bar features dapper bartenders, and, as is the case at many old-school joints, there isn't a drink menu. The dimly lit space is a step back in time. Most of the hopping jazz clubs in Milwaukee that were located in the Bronzeville neighborhood during the 1940s and '50s have closed, leaving Caroline's one of only a few jazz clubs in the city.

Across the street is ❹ **Shaker's Cigar Bar,** Milwaukee's only licensed cigar bar, which has been an anchor in the neighborhood since it opened in 1986. It's also a speakeasy-themed lounge, restaurant, and live music venue. The building is rumored to be haunted, and the owner plays into the legend with magnificent stories and spooky tours of the basement and haunted penthouse. The penthouse is said to have been a brothel during Prohibition and is available for rentals.

Down the block is ❺ **Camino,** home of great burgers and an impressive American craft beer list. Camino also has 50-cent pierogi on Sunday nights and $5 burgers on Mondays, both popular with locals. On the corner is Zad's—a bar that couldn't get divier if it tried. If this is your thing, stop in for a tap—it's open in the morning too. Buy a T-shirt.

Craft breweries, distilleries, coffee shops, and creameries (this is Wisconsin) are all available along this stretch in Walker's Point. ❻ **Clock Shadow Creamery** is a small urban cheese factory and shop offering incredible cheese and cheese curds—a must-try when in Wisconsin. If they're squeaky when you bite into them, you know they're done right. The Clock Shadow Building is a source of pride for the neighborhood because it's a former brownfield site redeveloped into a completely sustainable structure.

At the intersection of South Second and Pierce Streets, check out the orange-and-black koi fish mural created by artist Jeremy Novy. Most likely you will see these stenciled koi all over town—on walls, on sidewalks, and even in frames.

The intersection of South Second Street and National Avenue is the heart of Walker's Point. On the northwest corner, ❼ **Cielito Lindo** serves authentic Mexican drinks and food, including *molcajete,* which is a rare, meat-heavy menu item in Milwaukee Mexican restaurants and done particularly well here. Just try not to load up too much on the free chips and salsa first. Across National Avenue, ❽ **LaCage** has been in business for 40 years, making it Milwaukee's longest-running LGBTQ nightclub. Located inside a historic 1886 building, it features a large nightclub; a lower-level bistro; and event space for weddings, events, and performances on the top floor. Because of its long-standing success, gorgeous facade, and consistent updating of the nightclub, LaCage is definitely the crown jewel of The Gayborhood. ❾ **Steny's,** on the southeast corner, is an iconic motorcycle and sports bar known for its simple but delicious Bloody Mary.

A couple of doors down on Second, ❿ **Walker's Pint** is one of the only lesbian/women's bars left in the country. It's true most have closed in the past decade, but The Pint remains a fun party spot with weekly DJs and karaoke, as well as a spirited sports bar. It also hosts fundraisers for oodles of good causes in Milwaukee and is inclusive of everyone—as long as they're nice.

Keep walking south toward the Polish Moon. On the right, ⓫ **Crazy Water,** an American-fusion restaurant and one of the first foodie places to open in the neighborhood, continues to stand proud and waft its great smells over neighboring homes. Its quaint, intimate interior and patio draw people from all over the city for special occasions. The most amazing aspect of Crazy Water is how many different scrumptious meals come out of the tiny bar-side kitchen, including salmon, steak, and the signature Crazy Shrimp. The space was formerly Zur Krone, a German-themed bar known for serving beer in glass boots.

When you arrive at ⓬ **Rockwell Automation,** formerly Allen-Bradley, look up at the massive four-sided clock towering over the neighborhood. It was the largest in the world from 1962 until Saudi Arabia's Abraj Al Bait clock was completed in 2010. It's possible to get a tour of the tower by calling ahead. Turn around and start walking north, with the Polish Moon now at your back.

At West Washington Street, take a right and head east, crossing South First Street, to ⓭ **Don's,** a kitschy diner and bar with comfort food items and boozy shakes. Turn right and check out the cluster of former industrial buildings, which house a few eclectic antiques shops. Turn left at the next corner, on East Scott Street, then left (north) on South Barclay Street. Now you're on the edge of the Harbor District, near the confluence of Milwaukee's three rivers and once the center of southeastern Wisconsin's economic prosperity. Back at Washington Street turn right; you'll pass a trailhead for the Kinnickinnic River Trail and walk under a railroad bridge to a large cul-de-sac. Everything here is private property, but be sure to walk up to the fences and look past the remaining active industry to the water and, just beyond that, Jones Island, where, depending on the time of year, you can glimpse a sea of shipping containers or mountains of salt.

Jones Island, which is actually a peninsula, was once home to a large immigrant population of fisher folk. Made up predominantly of Kashubes, an ancient people from what is now northern Poland, Jones Island's fishing community worked Lake Michigan for decades until forced off the island to make way for the city's wastewater treatment plant.

Try the Bloody Mary at Steny's sports and biker bar.

The plant is also where lawn fertilizer Milorganite is made; that's what accounts for the sometimes less-than-flowery smell of the neighborhood. The Milwaukee-made fertilizer, a byproduct of wastewater treatment, has been on the market since the 1920s and has sold more than 4 million metric tons since its inception, but it's also the butt of many local jokes. Pun intended (sorry). Let's just hope you're walking with the wind at your back as you turn left and walk north. This is what's alternately referred to as South Water Street or the Kinnickinnic River Trail.

Up ahead, more renovated industrial spaces on your right now house casual yet elegant ⑭ **Boone & Crockett,** a popular cocktail lounge on the edge of the river. The decor features furniture and a bar made from rustic reclaimed wood, vintage chandeliers, lamps made from gramophone, and taxidermy art. It's connected to a concert venue and event space called The Cooperage. Across the street on the corner is Kruz, an LGBTQ bar and nightclub with a patio packed with beautiful, blooming plants in the summertime.

Continue walking in a northerly direction as aptly named South Water Street follows the contours of first the Kinnickinnic River and then the Milwaukee River. You'll get a better look at the mouth of Milwaukee's harbor at the Milwaukee County Boat Launch, surrounded by boat storage facilities in an old warehouse district. Across the water, enjoy a spectacular view of the bright-yellow Daniel Hoan Bridge, named after Milwaukee's second Socialist mayor. Warehouses and old industrial spaces turn to newer theaters, condos, and frozen-yogurt shops as you continue to follow the river. If it's summertime, ⑮ **Milwaukee Kayak Company** provides rentals to further explore Milwaukee's inner harbor from the water.

Cross South First Street and head west down East Seeboth Street to where it looks like it ends at the railroad tracks. Just on the left ahead is a pedestrian walkway that goes (barely) underneath the tracks. We hope a freight train is traveling overhead so you get the full sensory experience! Once past the tracks, go to the end of the block, turn right on South Second Street, and walk back to your starting point.

Boone & Crockett is a popular riverside cocktail lounge with a unique vintage atmosphere.

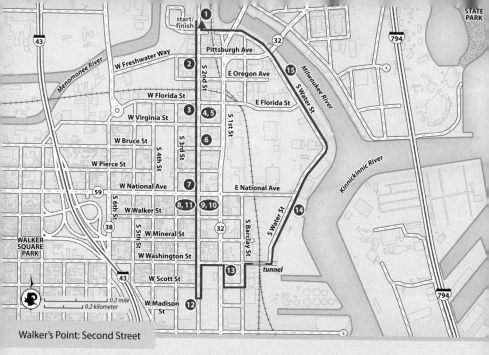

Walker's Point: Second Street

Points of Interest

1 Lindsay Building 126 S. Second St.

2 Purple Door Ice Cream 205 S. Second St., 414-988-2521, purpledooricecream.com

3 Caroline's Jazz Club 401 S. Second St., 414-221-9444, facebook.com/CarolinesJazzClub

4 Shaker's Cigar Bar 422 S. Second St., 414-272-4222, shakerscigarbar.com

5 Camino 434 S. Second St., 414-800-5641, caminomke.com

6 Clock Shadow Creamery 138 W. Bruce St., 414-273-9711, clockshadowcreamery.com

7 Cielito Lindo 733 S. Second St., 414-649-0401, cielitolindomilwaukee.com

8 LaCage 801 S. Second St., 414-383-8330, facebook.com/LaCageNiteclub

9 Steny's, 800 S. Second St., 414-672-7139, stenystavern.com/home.php

10 Walker's Pint 818 S. Second St., 414-643-7468, walkerspint.com

11 Crazy Water 839 S. Second St., 414-645-2606, crazywatermilwaukee.com

12 Rockwell Automation/Allen-Bradley Clock 1201 S. Second St., 414-382-2000, rockwellautomation.com

13 Don's Diner 1100 S. First St., 414-808-0805, donsmke.com

14 Boone & Crockett 818 S. Water St., 414-212-8115, boonemilwaukee.com

15 Milwaukee Kayak Company 318 S. Water St., 414-301-2240, milwaukeekayak.com

12 Walker's Point: Fifth Street
Motorcycles and Bottomless Baskets of Chips

Above: The second location of Fuel Cafe, serving everything from sandwiches to Korean bowls

BOUNDARIES: W. Canal St., W. Washington St., S. Fifth St., S. Sixth St.
DISTANCE: Approximately 2.25 miles
DIFFICULTY: Easy
PARKING: Street parking at S. Fifth St. and W. Washington St.
PUBLIC TRANSIT: MCTS route 80; stop is on S. Sixth St. at W. Washington St., 1 block west of start.

This part of the Walker's Point neighborhood is grittier, more industrial, and in the midst of a massive revival. It's a confluence of biker culture, LGBTQ culture, and Latino culture, with the recent addition of craft breweries, art galleries, and locally owned and operated shops.

Milwaukee is the birthplace of Harley-Davidson motorcycles, so biker culture is particularly revered here. The company's 100-year celebration in 2003 was the largest citywide party in history and has been replicated every five years since the inaugural bash. The festivities take place all over the city but are heavily concentrated in this area because of its moto-themed Fuel Cafe (there is also a Fuel Cafe in the Riverwest neighborhood) and the Harley-Davidson Museum.

If motorcycles don't rev your engine, there's plenty else to see and do in this historic-meets-hip part of Milwaukee.

Walk Description

Begin on South Fifth Street at ❶ **Arts @ Large,** an organization of artist-educators who, with students as well as emerging and established artists, work to promote creativity in the city. It was renovated and relocated from up the street to this historic building in 2019. There is an adjoining café, featuring locally roasted Anodyne Coffee, locally made Purple Door ice cream, and a handful of other menu items. The café also sells the creations of about 20 artists.

Head north along South Fifth Street to West National Avenue, where ❷ **Botanas** is a popular, long-standing Mexican eatery. In addition to the city's well-known history of beer production, among its lesser-known aspects is its large Mexican American population. Milwaukee is home to scores of incredible Mexican restaurants boasting bottomless baskets of chips and salsa, as well as extensive margarita offerings. Botanas, the last of what was once the "big three" of Mexican restaurants on South Fifth Street, offers these things plus entrées with different combinations of tacos, burritos, enchiladas, chimichangas, flautas, and tamales.

Cross National Avenue and continue north on Fifth Street. ❸ **Hamburger Mary's** is an LGBTQ-themed "classy-kitsch" diner and bar with entertainment, including drag shows, drag queen bingo, and retro video games in Mary's Beer Arcade. There is also a rooftop patio. Although it doesn't feel like a chain restaurant, there are 16 Hamburger Mary's franchises, with locations in Chicago, Denver, Houston, Ontario, Orlando, Saint Louis, San Francisco, and West Hollywood.

On the next block, the motorcycle-themed ❹ **Fuel Cafe** offers breakfast, hearty sandwiches, chili, wings, and Korean bowls. Fuel also has a full bar, a café/bakery, and a fun patio. The original Fuel Cafe opened in 1993 in the Riverwest neighborhood, serving as the first Seattle-style coffee shop in Milwaukee. This location opened in 2016 and has a similar vibe but is slightly more deluxe in decor and has a larger menu. The Cheesy Tomato sandwich—available at both locations—is on the short list of sammies adored by locals.

Note the mural across the street of the deceased, beloved pop star Selena Quintanilla-Pérez, known to her fans as Selena. Local artist Mauricio Ramirez used spray paint and tape to create the 20-by-50-foot conceptual piece.

Walker's Point welcomed ❺ **Walker's Lounge** in September 2019. The lounge, set inside a building that was once a Cuban mojito bar and, before that, a club called Hemingway's, still features much of the ornate decor, including dazzling chandeliers, hardwood flooring, and a gargantuan hand-carved bar. Walker's Lounge is open for dinner most nights and brunch—which includes bottomless mimosas—on the weekends.

Head north to West Virginia Street, where local ❻ MobCraft Brewery and Taproom is on the left. This is MobCraft's second location—the other is in Madison—and it's inside a 1945 former industrial building. Both are crowd-sourced breweries, which in this case means they hold online contests to determine what to brew. Brewers and beer lovers from around the world submit concepts and recipes, the public votes, and the winners are bottled and sold. They've made many unusual beers, including a Booze Cruise pineapple-and-mango saison, a Vanilla Wafer chocolate-vanilla porter, and a Jalapeño Hopper ale. MobCraft is believed to be the only brewery of this nature in the world.

Veer left to follow the roundabout and continue north on South Sixth Street. Although roundabouts are prevalent in the suburbs, this one is forever a source of conversation, and consternation, for Milwaukeeans. Be careful when crossing. On the right, ❼ The Iron Horse Hotel is a motorcycle-themed boutique hotel that opened in 2009 inside a former mattress factory that was originally built in 1907. The name refers to a Victorian term for a steam locomotive and is also a nickname for motorcycles. The boutique hotel celebrates riding, bike history and culture, food, art, and music. It's also one of Milwaukee's few dog-friendly hotels. Almost all of the decor is made from recycled, reused, or repurposed materials. There are two restaurants inside, Ash and Branded. The large patio, called The Yard, features communal fire pits, modern lounge furniture, a custom steel-and-wood pergola, a wood-fired cooking pit, and a full outside bar. The hotel's lobby is open to the public and worth a visit—if for no other reason than to see a huge art piece of the American flag made from 32½ pairs of Wrangler jeans.

Walk onto the Sixth Street Viaduct, and then take the pedestrian ramp down from the bridge toward West Freshwater Way. This is a leg on the Hank Aaron State Trail. Follow the trail along the Menomonee River canal, using West Freshwater Way as your return route to the viaduct. The natural plantings here along the canal are part of the Reed Street Yards, a city-financed project of water recycling, bioswales, and other stormwater-runoff reclamations.

Go back up the ramp to the sidewalk on the bridge, and continue north across the canal. Take a right onto the ❽ Harley-Davidson Museum property. Walk the middle of the grounds or follow the paths around the museum buildings next to the water (this is another leg on the Hank Aaron State Trail), then head inside. The museum, which opened in 2008, is accessible 363 days a year. It features galleries and exhibits that showcase Harley-Davidson motorcycles, from the very first examples to those hot off the line. It also hosts events, including regular Bike Nights,

The Harley-Davidson Museum displays bikes and parts spanning the company's 117-year history.

concerts, festivals, and tours (including a Steel Toe Tour with a bus trip off-site to the Harley-Davidson Powertrain Operations Facility in Menomonee Falls, where engines and transmissions are made). The complex also offers a restaurant and café called Motor and a gift shop with collectibles, clothing, and souvenirs.

Exit the museum property at the West Canal Street traffic light, crossing South Sixth Street. Take a left (south) to walk back on South Sixth Street, now on the west side. After crossing the viaduct, follow the roundabout again to West Virginia Street.

Milwaukee's first distillery that opened after Prohibition, **9 Great Lakes Distillery,** is located to the right (west) of the roundabout. Great Lakes is the home of Rehorst vodka, one of Milwaukee's favorite small-batch vodkas, among other spirits. There's also a patio, a gift shop, and an open-to-the-public tasting room with food.

The mosaic sculpture on top of the Coakley Brothers building—a commercial and residential moving business—was created by a Brooklyn-based artist in 2017. Made of Plexiglas, plastic, and steel, it sits where the building's original water tower stood and is intended to look like a kaleidoscope-patterned water tower, in homage to the one that was removed.

Iconic hole-in-the-wall Mexican cantina **10 Conejito's** is opposite the distillery on the southeast corner of the intersection. Step inside to sample cheap Mexican comfort food served on paper plates and short, tart margaritas. Note the extensive rabbit iconography—*conejito* means "bunny" in Spanish—and the plantless pots hanging from the ceiling.

Continue south along South Sixth Street. Check out the fun dichotomy of upscale Hotel Madrid on your left and the dive bar Camacho's across the street. While two very different crowds assemble at each, there is nothing preventing an open-minded walker from stopping in at both.

⓫ Zócalo is Milwaukee's first food truck park. Mazorca taco truck, Fontelle's Eatery (burgers and fries), Scratch Scoop Shop (ice cream), Ruby's Bagel's, Anytime Arepa, and Foxfire are circled up like wagons around outdoor eating and live performance spaces and two bars, one a former garage on the alley, and a central tavern space designed by local artist Gloria Ruiz-Santos.

On the next corner with National Avenue is another recent addition to the neighborhood, Walker's Point Music Hall, a bar and live music venue. To the right, two doors down the block on National Avenue is **⓬ La Casa de Alberto.** Opened by former employees of Conejito's, Alberto and Laura Gonzalez also offer Mexican comfort food and good margaritas as well as other items never featured on the menu at their former restaurant of 18 years, like fajitas and shrimp diablo.

The Mercantile Lofts, formerly Esperanza Unida, is the large building on the southwest corner of the intersection. Across the entire south-facing wall, clearly visible to travelers on I-43 above, is the **⓭ Mural of Peace.** The mural was completed by Reynaldo Hernandez in 1993 with the help of his children. In a story for WUWM, Milwaukee's public radio, Hernandez is quoted as saying the building owner who commissioned his work gave him instructions "to show the diversity of the south side of Milwaukee and show its aspirations and concerns." Hernandez responded with his image of a peace dove and other larger-than-life elements that stretch across the entire building.

"The whole world has the same concerns, like we all want happiness, we all hope for peace," says Hernandez, responding to the request to focus on the South Side.

Take a left on West Walker Street, heading a block east back to South Fifth Street. On the corner is the **⓮ Walker's Point Center for the Arts,** a gallery and education center serving the community for more than 30 years. Among myriad other shows and events, it hosts the popular Día de los Muertos annual altar exhibit.

Take a right on South Fifth Street. In the middle of the block north of West Washington Street is **⓯ Voces de la Frontera,** an immigrant and workers rights center originally founded in Texas in 1994. In addition to statewide election and political action and opposing ICE raids, the organization's annual May Day parade and Day Without Latinos events have brought tens of thousands of people out to the streets for racial equality and social and economic justice.

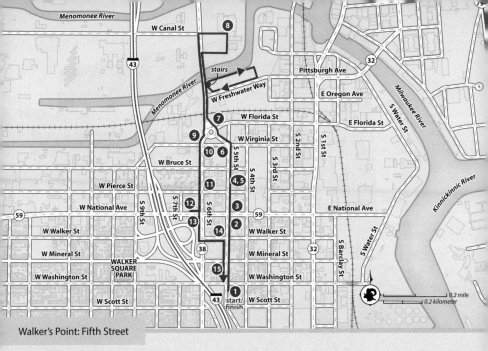

Walker's Point: Fifth Street

Points of Interest

1 **Arts @ Large** 1100 S. Fifth St., 414-763-7379, artsatlargeinc.org

2 **Botanas Restaurant** 816 S. Fifth St., 414-672-3755, botanasoriginal.com

3 **Hamburger Mary's** 730–734 S. Fifth St., 414-488-2555, hamburgermarys.com/mke

4 **Fuel Cafe** 630 S. Fifth St., 414-847-9580, fuelcafe.com

5 **Walker's Lounge** 626 S. Fifth St., 414-312-7563, facebook.com/walkersmke

6 **MobCraft Brewery** 505 S. Fifth St., 414-488-2019, mobcraftbeer.com

7 **The Iron Horse Hotel** 500 W. Florida St., 414-374-4766, theironhorsehotel.com

8 **Harley-Davidson Museum** 400 W. Canal St., 877-436-8738, harley-davidson.com

9 **Great Lakes Distillery** 616 W. Virginia St., 414-431-8683, greatlakesdistillery.com

10 **Conejito's Place** 539 W. Virginia St., 414-278-9106, conejitos-place.com

11 **Zócalo** 636 S. Sixth St., 414-433-9747, zocalomke.com

12 **La Casa de Alberto** 624 W. National Ave., 414-643-5715

13 *Mural of Peace* Mercantile Lofts, 611 W. National Ave.

14 **Walker's Point Center for the Arts** 839 S. Fifth St., 414-672-2787, wpca-milwaukee.org

15 **Voces de la Frontera** 1027 S. Fifth St., 414-643-1620, vdlf.org

13 West Historic Mitchell Street
Minowakiing and the Polish Grand Avenue

Above: Transfer Pizzeria Café, located inside a former pharmacy

---

BOUNDARIES: W. Historic Mitchell St., W. Maple St., S. First St., W. Forest Home Ave.
DISTANCE: Approximately 2 miles
DIFFICULTY: Easy
PARKING: Street parking near Transfer Pizzeria Café
PUBLIC TRANSIT: An MCTS hub is across from the walk start: Routes 15, 17, 54, and the Green Line
   stop here; routes 19 and 80 cross the walk farther west.

Milwaukee is home to many Mitchells, most of them named after Alexander Mitchell, a Scottish immigrant turned railroad baron who, by the middle of the 19th century, was the wealthiest man in the state: the opulent Mitchell Building, in downtown Milwaukee; the Mitchell Park Domes, one of the city's most popular attractions, with three beehive-shaped glass domes filled with plants and flowers; and Historic Mitchell Street, which is the heart of Milwaukee's South Side.

The West Historic Mitchell Street neighborhood was predominantly built up by Polish families from the 1800s through the 1960s. They opened many shops and small businesses where Polish was the preferred, if not the only, language. St. Stanislaus Church, perhaps the most notable in a street full of landmarks, was built for and by Polish Catholic immigrants in 1872.

During the first three-quarters of the 20th century, Mitchell Street was the busiest shopping district on the South Side. Known as the Polish Grand Avenue after the bustling downtown commercial street (now called Wisconsin Avenue), Mitchell featured numerous theaters, a Schuster's department store; a nearby Sears, Roebuck & Co.; and the iconic Goldmann's department store. It also became the go-to street for brides-to-be in search of the perfect wedding dress.

Today, Mexican Americans are the largest cultural group in the neighborhood. More than half of the residents speak Spanish as their first language. But local author and radio producer Adam Carr once documented that every continent is represented on Mitchell Street: Australians, European and African Americans, and immigrants from Southeast Asia and Middle Eastern nations join their Mexican American and American Indian neighbors.

The Ojibwe, Ottawa (Odawa), Menominee, and Potawatomi were the four largest First Nations peoples in what is now Milwaukee when French fur traders arrived in the 1670s. The Potawatomi maintain the largest presence in present-day Milwaukee, most prominently with the Potawatomi Hotel and Casino in nearby Menomonee Valley, but Indians with many tribal affiliations live across the city.

As University of Wisconsin–Milwaukee professor Margaret Noodin clarifies, in the language of the Anishinaabe People, or the People of the Three Fires (Ojibwe, Odawa, and Potawatomi), *Milwaukee,* or rather *Minowakiing,* does indeed mean "Good Land."

Walk Description

Start the walk at ❶ **Transfer Pizzeria Café,** heading west. Located inside a former pharmacy complete with lunch counter, the contemporary pizza shop became a Milwaukee staple in the past decade.

After walking a few blocks, over the I-94 freeway, note ❷ **St. Stanislaus Church,** the first Polish church in America. It was constructed with Cream City brick, a light-colored brick made from clay from the nearby Menomonee Valley. West Historic Mitchell Street has more than 10 times as many religious organizations per square mile than the average for Wisconsin.

Continue walking west on Historic Mitchell Street, taking in the vibrancy of the busy blocks. Window shopping is a viable pastime here. Just beyond the storefronts and extending up

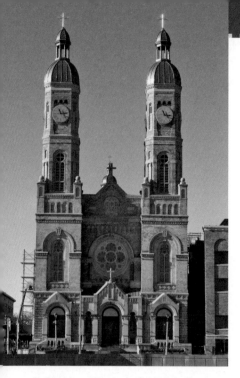

St. Stanislaus Church, the first Polish church in the United States

South Seventh Street is the ❸ **Kunzelmann-Esser Lofts** building, formerly home of a long-standing furniture company during Mitchell Street's first commercial heyday in the 20th century. The buildings of other old shopping powerhouses have made similar transitions to housing, such as part of the Schuster's department store building four blocks west.

Because of the large Latino population, many of the Historic Mitchell Street stores cater to this community with Mexican candy shops, restaurants, hair salons, and dress shops that stock quinceañera and first communion attire along with wedding gowns. Indian and Pakistani restaurants, as well as Milwaukee's only Syrian restaurant, are layered in the cultural mix of West Historic Mitchell Street.

❹ **Anmol** is a family-owned, traditional Pakistani restaurant. Signature dishes include mango-habanero chicken and a Pakistani fish fry. There is a second location in Chicago.

❺ **Damascus Gate,** Milwaukee's only Syrian restaurant, opened in 2018 and quickly became a fan favorite of people who love falafel, hummus, lentil soup, eggplant, and lamb. All the food is made from scratch by the owners with help from seven other Somali and Syrian refugees. The photos on the wall are of pre–Civil War Syria and offer hope for a better future.

The ❻ **Mitchell Street Library,** built in 2017, is the largest branch library in Milwaukee, second in size only to the Central Library downtown. Its contemporary decor includes mod furniture, a fireplace, a mezzanine, and both classic and cutting-edge materials. There is also a maker space on the lower level of the building. This library is particularly supportive of local arts and houses an artist-in-residence.

❼ **Gerald L. Ignace Indian Health Center** provides a variety of health services to all but focuses on the urban American Indian population. The renovated space formerly housed Goldmann's, once Wisconsin's oldest department store, which lived well past its heyday, keeping the classic lunch counter going until 2007, as well as its store specialties (or peculiarities) in stock, ranging from a classic candy counter selling retro sweets like jawbreakers and candy raisins to racks of school uniforms, zoot suits, African clothing sets, stacks of flour sack towels, an extensive selection of shopping carts, unique lights and lampshades, bolts of fabric, and fake fur coats.

8 Lopez Bakery & Restaurant is a classic *panadería* also serving scratch-made Mexican lunch plates. The M&M cookies alone warrant a stop, and you can still get three small loaves of *pan* for $1.

Right next door is **9 Scout Gallery,** owned by a husband-and-wife artist team. Opened in 2019 with a mission to be a part of the neighborhood while also connecting beyond it, Scout exhibits and sells inventive contemporary art and provides studio space for exceptional local artists.

The **10 Modjeska Theater** is currently closed but is ripe for a revival. So far, efforts to restore the 1924 theater have not been successful, but there is much buzz about the future of the space. The original theater, built in 1910 on the same site, was named after Polish actor Helena Modjeska and featured vaudeville. By the final decades of the 20th century, the Modjeska stopped showing films but still served as a live music venue, notorious for its stage collapsing during a 1992 They Might Be Giants concert. (Luckily, no one was severely injured.)

Take a slight left on West Forest Home Avenue, where it meets Historic Mitchell and South 13th Street at an angle. Walk another quarter block on South 13th to take a left on West Maple Street.

Walk east on West Maple Street, the other side of the blocks you just traversed. As you go, note the general age of the structures around you and the presence of the angled streets: Forest Home, which you were on briefly, and West Windlake Avenue, five blocks ahead. Milwaukee has a

Over the years, the now-closed Modjeska Theater showcased vaudeville and contemporary concerts.

number of such streets—each radiating out from nearer the city's center across the usual grid—that provide interesting variations in the direction of housing and in shapes of the blocks they cut.

Like other once predominately Polish areas of town, housing stock in the Historic Mitchell Street neighborhood is primarily one- and two-story wood-frame houses and Polish flats, discussed in more detail on other walks. For now just be on the lookout for the raised foundations on these, as well as the doors on the lower level that often seem a little too short. One such flat was briefly the ⑪ **home of poet Lorine Niedecker**—called the Emily Dickinson of the 20th century—at 539 W. Maple St. Growing up and living mostly in Fort Atkinson, Wisconsin, Niedecker penned poetry primarily about nature, but she also wrote about Milwaukee's South Side while living here with her husband, Albert Millen, who worked in Cudahy at the Ladish Drop Forge. Another house the couple shared stands a few blocks down South Sixth Street with a plaque commemorating the poet tacked to the front porch.

On the other side of the freeway, ⑫ **Triskele's** is a cozy, women-owned bistro and bar that is considered a hidden gem by locals who frequent it. The inside features an open kitchen just behind the bar, where guests can watch one of the owners prepare meals while they enjoy Wisconsin craft beer served up by the other owner. In the ambient dining area, patrons rave about the mac and cheese, mussels, and burgers. One block east, the 1921 ⑬ **Parts House Lofts** is an early example of Milwaukee's old commercial spaces renovated for other purposes, this one for condominiums in the early 2000s. Take a left on South First Street and walk one block back to Transfer Pizzeria Café. Consider stopping in for a traditional or specialty pie, such as the Milwaukee-famous Stacy's Special, with barbecue sauce, chicken, red onion, and smoked Gouda.

Connecting the Walks

Across South First Street is a trailhead for the Kinnickinnic River Trail, which you can take to join the Walker's Point: Second Street walk (page 60). Follow Maple Street another block and a half east, crossing South Kinnickinnic Avenue. Climb the paved ramp up a slight incline and take a left on the path that was formerly railway. This trail provides a back-of-town view formerly reserved for those riding Amtrak's *Hiawatha* commuter train into the city.

Triskele's menu offerings include craft beer, seasonal cocktails, mussels, and rave-worthy mac and cheese.

West Historic Mitchell Street

Points of Interest

1. **Transfer Pizzeria Café** 101 W. Mitchell St., 414-763-0438, transfermke.com

2. **St. Stanislaus Church** 524 W. Historic Mitchell St., 414-266-5490, institute-christ-king.org /milwaukee-home

3. **Kunzelmann-Esser Lofts** (private residences) 710 W. Historic Mitchell St.

4. **Anmol** 711 W. Historic Mitchell St., 414-672-7878, eatanmol.com

5. **Damascus Gate Restaurant** 807 W. Historic Mitchell St., 414-810-3561 damascusgatemilwaukee.com

6. **Milwaukee Public Library–Mitchell Street Branch** 906 W. Historic Mitchell St., 414-286-3000, mpl.org/hours_locations/mitchell.php

7. **Gerald L. Ignace Indian Health Center** 930 W. Historic Mitchell St., 414-383-9526, gliihc.net

8. **Lopez Bakery & Restaurant** 1100 W. Historic Mitchell St., 414-672-1830, lopez-bakery-restaurant.business.site

9. **Scout Gallery** 1104 W. Historic Mitchell St., contact via website, scoutgallerymke.com

10. **Modjeska Theater** (currently closed) 1134 W. Historic Mitchell St.

11. **Former home of poet Lorine Niedecker** (private residence) 539 W. Maple St.

12. **Triskele's** 1801 S. Third St., 414-837-5950, triskelesrestaurant.com

13. **Parts House Lofts** (private residences) 215 W. Maple St.

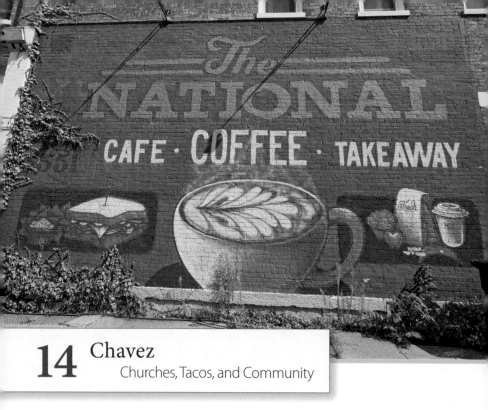

14 Chavez
Churches, Tacos, and Community

Above: The National Cafe in Walker's Point has some of the city's best ramen.

BOUNDARIES: W. Pierce St., W. Lapham Blvd., S. Seventh St., S. Cesar E. Chavez Dr.
DISTANCE: 3.5 miles
DIFFICULTY: Easy
PARKING: Free street parking
PUBLIC TRANSIT: MCTS route 19

Milwaukee is known as a city of churches, earning it one of its monikers, City of Steeples, and for having a grandiose number of bars in many neighborhoods. There's likely a number of different connections to be made between the proliferation of these two kinds of public spaces, but one of them is certainly a love of community.

Milwaukee is a city of immigrants, with a rich history and a multicultural present. Mexican immigrants have been arriving in the Walker's Point neighborhood since at least the 1920s and over the last 100 years moved west toward Clarke Square, where they joined English, Germans, Scots, Scandinavians, Eastern Europeans, and "Yankees" from the East Coast. Today, African American, Guatemalan, and Laotian Hmong families also live in the area covered by this walk.

The South Side is often depicted as the former stronghold of Polish immigrants and is now predominantly home to Mexican Americans. Multiethnic groups of immigrants have always made this area home, and some South Side neighborhoods remain pockets of multicultural, working-class life. This is one of them.

Walk Description

Start at ❶ **Taqueria El Cabrito** and order the *birria* (goat stew traditionally from the Mexican state of Jalisco); the cactus is also good. El Cabrito food trucks are located throughout Milwaukee's South Side—always a good choice for a quick taco on the go. Across the intersection is ❷ **St. Michael's Ukrainian Catholic Church,** which since the mid-20th century has been a site for Milwaukee's Ukrainian American Catholics to worship and socialize.

Head south on 11th Street, and then turn right on West Scott Street. The St. John Church of God in Christ (COGIC) is on the left. According to the organization's main offices in Tennessee, COGIC is a predominantly African American Pentecostal church founded in 1907 by Bishop Charles Harrison Mason. On the next block is Saint Mary's Ukrainian Orthodox Church; formerly Norwegian Lutheran, in 1917 it became the first cultural center for Ukrainian American immigrants in the city. On the next corner sits a girls' middle school, the Blessed Theresa Campus of the Notre Dame School of Milwaukee.

Turn left on South 14th Street and then right on West Greenfield Avenue. Iglesia de Dios Pentecostal, MI, or the Pentecostal Church of God, is an 1887 clapboard, balloon-frame building with an attached school building. Built by German immigrants, it originally housed the Zion Evangelical Church.

The building with the appealing modern sign reading ICON houses a men's clothing store. Ahead, on the other side of this oddly shaped intersection of three busy streets, is ❸ **Pete's Fruit Market.** Greek immigrant Pete Tsitiridis first set up an open-air market on this corner in 1992 after selling his first store in Waukegan, Illinois, and moving to Milwaukee. As its website proclaims, Pete's has always catered to its culturally diverse neighborhood, expanding numerous times over the years and recently adding a second location in the North Side neighborhood of Bronzeville (Walk 5, page 26).

Turn right (north) on South Cesar E. Chavez Drive. One of the commercial hubs for Milwaukee's Latino communities, Chavez Drive is home to numerous restaurants, grocery and Western-wear stores, more churches and social services, and a stop of the Tornado Bus Company, which has regular routes across the United States and Mexico.

4 **Taqueria Los Comales,** on the right, is a regional restaurant chain that Camerino Gonzalez started in Chicago's Little Village, first serving up "Mexico City–style tacos on a tiny grill" and expanding to more than 20 locations in three states.

A few blocks up, **5** **El Rey** is a family-owned chain of grocery stores that's been around since 1978. After Heriberto and Ernesto Villarreal moved to Milwaukee from Mexico, they opened a small grocery store to accommodate the growing Mexican population in Milwaukee. When immigrants from Central America, South America, and the Caribbean started to arrive, El Rey expanded its offerings to honor the tastes of the entire Latino population. Today there are three El Rey locations, known for their fresh and affordable produce, made-from-scratch tamales, colorful piñatas dangling from the ceiling, and sit-down eateries serving some of the city's best tacos and other Mexican eats.

Turn right on West Pierce Street, which is often considered the border of the Menomonee Valley neighborhood, as the historic river bluff begins its gradual slope down here. The **6** **Paper Box Lofts** building, constructed in 1920, features renovated apartments inside the building of the former Milwaukee company that made decorative packaging primarily for confectionery businesses in the United States, Europe, and China until 1938.

7 **Antiques on Pierce** is the largest antiques mall in southeastern Wisconsin with three floors and 90,000 square feet of space. The items for sale are a mix of vintage and new, including glassware, retro furniture, lighting, postcards, signs, books, maps, clothing, jewelry, sports and beer memorabilia, record albums, and more.

Turn right on South 11th Street and left on West National Avenue.

On the northeast corner of Ninth Street and National Avenue, **8** **Milwaukee Area Technical College's Walker's Point campus** offers construction and other trade and apprenticeship programs, including plumbing, tool-making, and masonry.

For more than 10 years, **9** **The National Cafe** has offered quality food—including meat or veggie sandwiches and popular tonkotsu ramen—along with a community meetup space in a hip environment.

Turn right (south) on South Ninth Street, and then turn right again on West Walker Street. **10** **Guadalajara** is a third-generation, family-owned Mexican restaurant serving family recipes in an 1890 space that feels like a living room with an antique, dark-wood bar. The homemade sopes, quesadillas, and dessert items are the stars of this menu.

Turn left on South 10th Street. At West Mineral Street, cross over to ⓫ **Walker Square Park,** one of Milwaukee's first three neighborhood parks established by the city's cofounder George Walker. It hosts many community events, including a Día de los Muertos celebration and a farmers market. Take the wide path that runs diagonally through the park from Mineral to the corner of South Ninth Street and West Washington Street.

The United Community Center houses health programs, community services, two charter schools, athletics (including a world-famous boxing program), and ⓬ **Café el Sol,** offering Puerto Rican and Mexican cuisine and Milwaukee's only Latin-style fish fry on Friday nights.

From the park, cross Ninth Street and then Washington Street to the tranquil Mother Mary statue and grotto. From the grotto continue south on Ninth Street and then left on West Scott Street, where Apostolic Pentecostal Church stands. Originally home to a Norwegian Lutheran congregation since at least 1858, the current structure was dedicated in 1895.

Turn left (north) on South Eighth Street. Christ–St. Peter Lutheran School, a collaboration between Christ Lutheran Church and St. Peter Lutheran Church, is on both sides of the street. St. Peter Lutheran Church was established in 1885. It later joined forces with Christ Evangelical Lutheran Church about 1 mile west. Both are dedicated to serving English-, Spanish- and Karen-speaking Christians.

Turn right (east) on West Washington Street. Along this block are Catholic Charities buildings, including Immigrant Legal Services, with St. Patrick's Church on the corner. Originally an Irish church and school, the congregation has a history of welcoming immigrants, first from Germany and Slovenia in the 1950s, and later from Spanish-speaking countries.

Turn right (south) on South Seventh Street. At the corner of Madison and Seventh, Iglesia Evangelica Bautista is a Spanish-speaking Baptist church. On the next corner is Super Taqueria Don Pancho, which doesn't have a liquor license but does have excellent burritos. Its brightly painted building was the original site of Maria's Pizza, which you'll visit on the Jackson Park walk (page 147).

Turn right (west) on West Greenfield Avenue. The imposing Cream City brick structure looming ahead is currently ⓭ **La Causa Early Education & Care Center.** Built in 1879, the location was formerly the St. Vincent's Infant Asylum, an orphanage that, according to records at the Archdiocese of Milwaukee, housed as many as 500 children at a time. Kids unadopted by age 7 were sent to other orphanages.

Turn left (south) on South Ninth Street and go two blocks to Lapham Boulevard. ⑭ **Bryant's Cocktail Lounge,** open since 1938, is a recently renovated but historically accurate lounge with ambient lighting, plush velvet walls, and old-school tunes that features hundreds of exotic cocktails—some of which include ice cream or flaming fruit—that are not listed on menus but are committed to memory by the staff. The Brain Buster, Bryant's boozy signature drink, is the most requested and definitely a "one and done" cocktail.

Turn right (west) on West Lapham Boulevard. ⑮ **The Congregation of the Great Spirit,** an American Indian Catholic church, combines native traditions with the teachings of Jesus Christ. The church is also a reminder of the continuing presence of the many native peoples in the neighborhood and across the city.

Turn right (north) on South 11th Street. The Wisconsin Division of Forensic Sciences' Milwaukee Laboratory analyzes physical evidence from crime scenes statewide.

Turn right (east) on West Greenfield Avenue, and then turn left on South 10th Street. The ⑯ **St. Vincent de Paul Society Meal Program** serves free hot meals six nights a week. The program also offers holiday events, shower facilities, and clean clothing. According to the organization, it served 89,000 meals in 2018, 15,311 of them to children.

Back at Walker Square Park, take a left on West Washington Street to return to the start.

Points of Interest

① Taqueria El Cabrito 1100 S. 11 St., 414-385-9000, facebook.com/elcabritotaqueria

② St. Michael's Ukrainian Church 1025 S. 11th St., 414-672-5616, stmichaelsukr.org

③ Pete's Fruit Market 1400 S. Union St., 414-383-1300, petesfruitmarket.com

④ Taqueria Los Comales 1306 S. Cesar E Chavez Dr., 414-384-6101, loscomales.com

⑤ El Rey 916 S. Cesar E Chavez Dr., 414-643-1640, elreyfoods.com

⑥ Paper Box Lofts 1560 W. Pierce St.

⑦ Antiques on Pierce 1512 W. Pierce St., 414-645-9640, antiquesonpierce.com

⑧ Milwaukee Area Technical College's Walker's Square Education Center 816 W. National Ave., 414-297-7923, matc.edu

Chavez

9 The National Cafe 839 W. National Ave., 414-431-6551, nationaleats.com

10 Guadalajara 901 S. 10th St., 414-647-2266, facebook.com/gdlmexicanfood

11 Walker Square Park 1031 S. Ninth St., countyparks.com

12 Café el Sol 1028 S. Ninth St., 414-384-3100, unitedcc.org/community-services/café-el-sol

13 La Causa Early Education & Care Center 809 W. Greenfield Ave., 414-647-8750, lacausa.org
/programs/early-education-care-center

14 Bryant's Cocktail Lounge 1579 S. Ninth St., 414-383-2620, bryantscocktaillounge.com

15 Congregation of the Great Spirit 1000 W. Lapham Blvd., 414-672-6989, archmil.org

16 St. Vincent de Paul Society Meal Program 931 W. Madison St., 414-649-9555, svdpmilw.org
/meal_program.aspx

15 Lakefront
A Great Place by a Great Lake

Above: McKinley Marina, adjacent to McKinley Beach, is the city's only public marina.

BOUNDARIES: E. Ravine Rd., E. Lagoon Dr., N. Lincoln Memorial Dr., N. Terrace Ave.
DISTANCE: 4.25 miles
DIFFICULTY: Difficult (walking the lake bluff can be challenging)
PARKING: Street parking along Lagoon Dr.
PUBLIC TRANSIT: MCTS routes 30 and the Gold Line on Prospect above Lagoon Dr. At the Prospect and Brady stop, take the Oak Leaf Trail down the lake bluff across the pedestrian bridge to Lagoon Dr.; alternatively, MCTS route 21 intersects the route at the midpoint at the North Point Water Tower.

In the 1980s, Milwaukee's tagline was "A Great Place by a Great Lake." This redundant but loved slogan is still commonly used in Milwaukee culture and vernacular today.

Lake Michigan is one of the five Great Lakes—along with Lake Superior, Lake Huron, Lake Ontario, and Lake Erie—and is the only one located entirely in the United States (the others border Canada). The word *Michigan* comes from the Anishinaabemowin (Ojibwe language) word *michi-gami,* meaning "great water."

Although 12 million people in Wisconsin, Illinois, Indiana, and Michigan live along the shores of Lake Michigan, which is known as The Third Coast, Milwaukeeans claim the lake entirely as their own. It's a beloved place for many—a massive, mystifying element that changes color and texture every day. Most Milwaukeeans go to the lake in search of leisure and recreation, but there's always a person or two sitting on the rocks or in their car, facing the extraordinary lake, reflecting.

The stretch of Lake Michigan that's in Milwaukee is 1,400 acres and includes beaches, parks, and green space next to the water, including Bradford Beach, which is located near downtown and was named one of the best city beaches in the United States by the Travel Channel. The winters are long in Milwaukee, so summertime infuses excitement into the air and inspires people to get out and do something. On these limited days the lake—particularly its beaches—acts as a magnet, drawing people from neighborhoods in all directions. Although people flock to the beach to bask in the sun, the sounds of the waves lapping against the rocks or the birds alerting each other that popcorn spilled in the parking lot are equally rewarding.

Walk Description

❶ **Veterans Park** commemorates military service with a court of honor and serves as a community spot to relax or get active in nature. The Milwaukee Community Sailing Center has taught more than 100,000 kids and adults how to sail since its inception in 1977 and is located on the east end of the park, as is a kite store that hosts an annual kite festival. Long paths on the water's edge and on part of the breakwater for McKinley Marina are available in the park, with plenty of grassy areas and tables for picnicking, playing Frisbee, or lounging.

Begin in Veterans Park on East Lagoon Drive opposite ❷ **Wheel Fun Rentals** at the lagoon, where you can rent canoes, kayaks, and pedal boats—some of which are swan-shaped. Other rental locations along the lakeshore also offer different styles of bicycles, from traditional bikes to surrey bikes that fit the whole family. Bikers can explore the Oak Leaf Trail, part of which is along the lakefront.

Leave the park on Lagoon Drive, crossing and taking a right on North Lincoln Memorial Drive. ❸ **Colectivo** is a locally owned café, pub, and eatery housed inside a Victorian Romanesque Revival–style building that was once the Milwaukee River Flushing Station. The building features Cream City brick, a prevalent clay-based building material named for its light color, and the 1912 flushing station pump—which is still operational—is on full display inside the café.

Colectivo has 13 cafés in metro Milwaukee, 5 in Chicago, and 3 in Madison; the Lakefront café was the second location. The river-flushing station is part of a project begun in 1887 to pull water out of Lake Michigan and, as its name implies, pump it up the bluff to the river to flush the once stagnant, polluted river water into the lake.

Take a left on East Lafayette Hill Road and head up the lake bluff. Climbing this hill gives an entirely new and wider perspective on the lake. On certain days, suddenly the ribbons of blue or green—or somewhere in between—on the lake's surface become more visible. Sometimes it's a wash of gray or a plate of sparkles. And always, it's impossible to believe that the lake doesn't stretch on forever.

Turn right to stay on East Lafayette Place, and continue following the contour of tiny Back Bay Park, taking a left on North Terrace Avenue.

On the right, ❹ Villa Terrace Decorative Arts Museum is an Italian Renaissance–style private home turned museum. It stores decorative arts from the 15th–19th centuries, including metalworks by Cyril Colnik, a Milwaukee ironsmith, and rotating exhibitions. It also features exquisite gardens that are open to the public. The Villa Terrace is a popular spot for weddings.

❺ North Point Water Tower is a Victorian Gothic–style tower that looks like it's straight out of a fairy tale. Even so, the magical-looking tower served the practical purpose of providing water to Milwaukeeans for 145 years. Inside, there's a steep, 213-step spiral staircase that's wide enough for only one person. Because of safety concerns, the water tower is not open to the public.

Today, the brick structure to the left of the tower is part of ❻ Ascension Columbia St. Mary's Hospital (the white buildings surrounding and across the street comprise the main hospital campus), but it was originally St. Mary's Hospital, which opened in 1858, with a new wing added in 1889. Some of Milwaukee's senior residents call it "the old St. Mary's" to this day.

The ❼ Frederick Bogk House, designed by Frank Lloyd Wright for Bogk, a city alderman and businessman, is Wright's only residential, single-family home in Milwaukee. Unlike many of Wright's projects, the house does not include Wright's well-known Prairie-style elements and is said to incorporate features of his designs for the Imperial Hotel in Tokyo.

Turn right on East Bradford Avenue and then left on North Wahl Avenue. ❽ North Point Lighthouse, built in 1866, is open to the public as a historical landmark and museum. Guests are invited to climb the 84 steps, free of charge, to the top of the lighthouse, on Saturdays and Sundays from 1 to 4 p.m.

Turn right on North Lake Drive and then right on East Newberry Boulevard. Here you can join the Upper East Side walk (Walk 4, page 20). Enter ❾ Lake Park, a 138-acre park on the lake designed in the late 19th century by Frederick Law Olmsted, who also designed Central Park in

New York City. (Milwaukeeans love this fact and share it readily.) It features the last remaining Indian mound in Milwaukee, natural landscaping, winding paths, bluffs, vistas, and wildlife, along with an 18-hole golf course. It also hosts a live music series in the summer, aptly named Music in the Park, and was an extremely popular PokéStop in the game Pokémon Go during the summer of 2016, which was controversial among the neighbors.

Turn left on North Lake Park Road; to the right are bocce courts in front of ❿ **Lake Park Bistro,** a French restaurant operated by the Bartolotta group, founded by the late Joe Bartolotta, a beloved restaurateur who worked in famous New York restaurants such as Tavern on the Green before returning to the Milwaukee area to open his own.

Follow Lake Park Road until it ends, and continue immediately on the park's path, which curves around to the left, past the Lake Park Summer Stage, and then back onto the park access road. Park buildings and the playground are on your left. At the end of the road, take a right on North Lincoln Memorial Drive.

The lake is mostly obscured by the trees until you reach a curve in the road and begin a long descent. There is little in the world that is more glorious than the simplicity in that moment when Lake Michigan comes into view.

The Lakefront location of Colectivo occupies an 1888 Victorian Revival–style building made of Cream City brick. The building was formerly the Milwaukee River Flushing Station.

The midcentury Bradford Pavilion, designed by county architect Gilbert Grunwald, has served generations of beachgoers at Bradford Beach.

Keep walking toward the beach at the bottom of the hill. Take a left, crossing North Lincoln Memorial Drive at the pedestrian walk located at the beach, and then right (south).

In about half a mile you'll come to ⓫ **Bradford Beach,** one of Milwaukee County's largest urban beaches. It offers cabana rentals, volleyball courts, summertime events, and concessions from The Dock, located inside the Bradford Pavilion. There's also a custard and burger stand called ⓬ **MooSa's** directly across the south parking lot. The name of this restaurant, painted like a cow, is a portmanteau of *moo* and the owner's name, Nas Musa, whose family also owns the local Casablanca restaurants on Brady Street and in the suburbs.

⓭ **McKinley Beach** is a smaller beach south of Bradford, with a playground for kids and picnic tables. Developed along with Bradford in the early 1900s, McKinley Beach is now a lesser-known, and therefore quieter, spot for relaxing on the sand.

The beach is next to ⓮ **McKinley Marina,** the only public marina in Milwaukee, featuring 655 boat slips. The breakwater, made from large stones removed from numerous Wisconsin quarries, runs out into the lake for half a mile to protect the marina and the boat launch from the open waters.

Next to the marina is the private ⓯ **Milwaukee Yacht Club.** It opened in 1871, making it the oldest yacht club on Lake Michigan. The clubhouse has a dining hall/restaurant, a bar and lounge, a pool, event space, and more.

Continue walking south along North Lincoln Memorial Drive back to Lagoon Drive.

Lakefront

Points of Interest

① **Veterans Park** 1010 N. Lincoln Memorial Dr., 414-257-7275, countyparks.com

② **Wheel Fun Rentals** 1400 N. Lincoln Memorial Dr., 414-232-5027, wheelfunrentals.com/wi /milwaukee/veterans-park-north

③ **Colectivo–Lakefront** 1701 N. Lincoln Memorial Dr., 414-223-4551, colectivocoffee.com

④ **Villa Terrace Decorative Arts Museum** 2220 N. Terrace Ave., 414-271-3656, villaterrace.org

⑤ **North Point Water Tower** 2288 N. Lake Dr., 414-286-2830, tinyurl.com/northpointtowermke

⑥ **Ascension Columbia St. Mary's Hospital** 2301 N. Lake Dr., 414-585-1000, healthcare.ascension.org

⑦ **Frederick Bogk House** (private residence) 2420 N. Terrace Ave.

⑧ **North Point Lighthouse** 2650 N. Wahl Ave., 414-332-6754, northpointlighthouse.org

⑨ **Lake Park** 3233 E. Kenwood Blvd., 414-257-7275, countyparks.com

⑩ **Bartolotta's Lake Park Bistro** 3133 E. Newberry Blvd., 414-962-6300, bartolottas.com/lake-park-bistro

⑪ **Bradford Beach** 2400 N. Lincoln Memorial Dr., 414-257-7275, countyparks.com

⑫ **MooSa's** 2272 N. Lincoln Memorial Dr., 414-727-4886, moosaburger.com

⑬ **McKinley Beach** 1750 N. Lincoln Memorial Dr., 414-257-7275, countyparks.com

⑭ **McKinley Marina** 1750 N. Lincoln Memorial Dr., 414-273-5224, countyparks.com

⑮ **Milwaukee Yacht Club** 1700 N. Lincoln Memorial Dr., 414-271-4455, milwaukeeyc.com

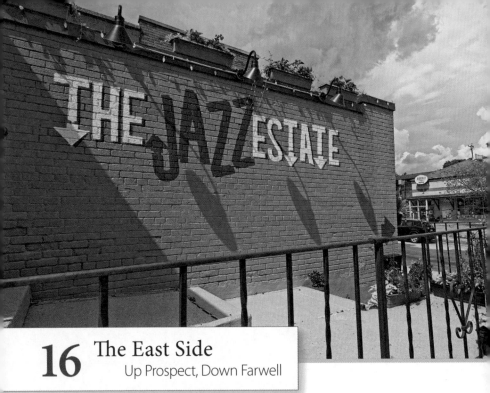

16 The East Side
Up Prospect, Down Farwell

Above: The Jazz Estate was immaculately remodeled in 2016.

BOUNDARIES: E. Greenwich Ave., E. Juneau Ave., N. Prospect Ave., N. Astor St.
DISTANCE: 3 miles
DIFFICULTY: Easy
PARKING: Limited street parking on E. Ogden Ave. or N. Astor St.
PUBLIC TRANSIT: MCTS route 30; The Hop streetcar: Ogden at Astor

---

Milwaukee's East Side was traditionally known as a college-kid hangout with plenty of bars to stumble into and places to chow down at bar time. Although this element still exists, the progressive neighborhood has evolved in the past few years. Today the neighborhood has as many upscale condos as it does college flops, and it offers the latest food trends as opposed to just the cheapest drinks. Of course, it's still possible to get a $3 pint (looking at you, Landmark Lanes) and a messy bar burger, but it's also a destination for sushi, live jazz music, small-plate dining, and a glass of wine in an opulent theater. Dare we say the East Side of Milwaukee is all grown up?

Walk Description

Start the walk at East Ogden Avenue and North Astor Street, and head south on Astor with the First Unitarian Society on your left. On the next block, you can't miss ❶ **County Clare** Irish inn and pub, a coral-pink building with shamrock green–painted trim. Since 1996, County Clare has brought authentic Irish culture to Milwaukee's East Side, including a pub and restaurant (cottage pie, please!), regular live music, and a hotel with 29 Euro-charming rooms and suites. Needless to say, a good pour of Guinness is just a few skips away at this point. *Sláinte!*

With the Astor Hotel on your right, make a left on East Juneau Avenue, and head toward ❷ **The Knickerbocker on the Lake** hotel, built in 1929. The stunning lobby reflects opulence with crystal chandeliers, a vaulted ceiling, and terrazzo floors, but despite its grandeur, The Knickerbocker on the Lake has a homey feel to it. This is in part because the Classical Revival boutique hotel is also the permanent residence of about 100 people. Yet it's very much a traveler's heaven: many of the rooms overlook Lake Michigan, as does the first-floor Lounge, called The Knick, which has an adjoining restaurant.

Cross North Prospect Avenue and note Juneau Park straight ahead (we explore Juneau Park in Walk 1, page 2). If you like, enter the park to see the 1947 replica of Solomon Juneau's cabin, based on a woodcut image of the 1822 original. Facing the park, turn left and head northeast. Burns Commons is on the left, prominently displaying a 16-foot statue of the Scottish poet Robert Burns. The statue was donated to Milwaukee in the early 20th century, but Milwaukee does not have any other ties to the man who quilled "Auld Lang Syne."

The ❸ **Jewish Museum Milwaukee** was founded in 2008, after archives had been collected since the 1980s, with a mission to explore Jewish history from local and global perspectives. Each year the museum curates two original exhibits and three temporary exhibits on loan from institutions worldwide. Milwaukee is home to about 20,000 Jews, more than half of whom live in the North Shore suburbs.

Located inside the McIntosh/Goodrich Mansion, the ❹ **Wisconsin Conservatory of Music,** offers private and small-group lessons in piano; stringed, percussion, woodwind, and brass instruments; and vocal arts in myriad styles. They even teach the harmonica!

Keep walking, past ❺ **The Shorecrest,** a nine-story, Moroccan/Art Deco–style structure that was built as a hotel in 1925 and today serves as an apartment building. From the 1970s until 2011, it was owned by members of the Balistrieri family. The original owner, Frank P. Balistrieri, was identified as Milwaukee's Mafia boss by federal authorities and in 1984 was convicted of extortion and sentenced to 13 years in prison. The restaurant on the ground floor has been many different concepts, most famously Snug's from 1977 to 1996.

Prospect transitions from primarily residential to primarily commerce at Kenilworth Place. With many shops, bars, restaurants, and services, this area is the heart of Milwaukee's bustling and trendy East Side. **6 Colectivo** coffee café is the local chain's original location, which opened in 1997. Today, there are 13 locations in Milwaukee, 3 in Madison, and 5 in Chicago. For many years, this café was also the roasting and wholesaling facility, which was moved to the location in the Riverwest neighborhood when that location opened in 2005. Colectivo–Prospect hosts the "Live from the Back Room at Colectivo" series, which welcomes local, national, and international musicians.

Turn left on North Maryland Avenue. On the right is **7 Maryland Avenue Montessori School,** a high-performing K-8 school that is part of the Milwaukee Public Schools (MPS) district. The original building was completed in 1893 but continues to expand and grow; a five-classroom addition went up in 2016. MPS has eight Montessori schools, which is the nation's largest number of public Montessori schools in one district.

Take a left on East Greenwich Avenue and then another left on North Murray Avenue. The Tool Shed is a woman-owned erotic shop with a great sense of humor and a dead-serious commitment to education and non-stigmatized sensual exploration.

Next door is **8 The Jazz Estate,** a vintage cocktail lounge and jazz club that's been around for almost 50 years but was spruced up a few years ago. The Jazz Estate hosts local and national acts and has a solid cocktail menu with staple and seasonal drinks. If the Wisconsin Old Fashioned (made with brandy instead of whiskey) is on your Milwaukee bucket list, this would be a fine place to cross it off the list.

9 Paddy's Pub is on Milwaukee's short list of authentic Irish bars. A married couple—yes, one of them is named Patty (the bar is spelled the Irish way)—opened the cozy pub in 1996. Paddy's is truly a "bigger on the inside" place, with four bars on two floors, multiple rooms, a few hallways, and a patio. Each room has its own feel, yet all are heavily adorned with antiques, Irish quotes, photos, and Celtic designs. Paddy's hosts lots of live music and Irish music sessions. It's truly always a lovely day for Paddy's Pub.

Cross East North Avenue, walking toward **10 Von Trier,** sometimes called Von Trier's because Milwaukeeans love to add an "s" to business names. This German-themed Milwaukee institution has been in operation since 1978. In 2017 the then-owner announced he was going to change from the old-world German theme to something more modern, and the community went into an outrage, circulating petitions and flocking to social media to demand it stay as is. And so it did.

To the left down North Avenue, notice Hooligan's Super Bar, another Milwaukee classic that's owned the tip of its triangular block since 1938. Hooli's has 30-plus taps, 12 TVs for sports watching, and a small kitchen known for huge local favorites like the Hooli burger and a variety of fish fries. When the patio is open in the summertime in front of the restaurant, it is literally the center of the East Side.

On the southeast corner, between Ivanhoe Place and Farwell Avenue, stands ⑪ **Crossroads Collective,** a popular food hall featuring new concepts along with walk-up versions of some of Milwaukee's most popular restaurants. The iconic space was the home of Oriental Drugs, a cherished drugstore with a storied, Asian-themed lunch counter. It was open from 1928 to 1995 and has been preserved by many local artists and writers who remember the eclectic spot fondly.

Take a right (southwest) on North Farwell Avenue. The ornate ⑫ **Oriental Theatre** was built in 1927 in a quirky mix of East Indian and Middle Eastern styles with ornate chandeliers, gold Buddha statues with glowing eyes, and artistic depictions of dozens—maybe hundreds—of lions and elephants. Once a single-screen theater with a balcony, the Oriental is now a triplex. The main theater remains the most stunning and has featured since its inception a house organ that a local musician plays before films. The organ had been removed after Landmark Theatres gave up the property, and its new tenants, Milwaukee Film, worked diligently to locate, restore, and install a replacement.

Black Cat Alley is a mural project featuring 17 murals (and growing) in the alley on the east side of this stretch of Farwell Avenue and is worth a detour. Landmark Lanes is a walk-down

The ornately decorated Oriental Theatre dates to 1927.

bar—actually three connected bars—along with a 16-lane bowling alley and an old-school arcade. It also has a hot pool scene, darts, karaoke, and more. Since the 1980s, Tuesday has been the big party night at the Landmark. Before the craft beer explosion, it was Import Night and, more recently, Pint Night.

⓭ **Ma Fischer's** is a classic Milwaukee diner. Because it's open 24 hours and close to so many bars, it's a hotbed of activity at bar time. In 2016, after 40 years of people walking in and asking, "So where's Ma?" the owners installed a 5-foot-8-inch statue of the former owner, Jackie Fischer— aka Ma—outside the building.

Keep walking southwest on Farwell, crossing the bridge over the Oak Leaf Trail. On the left, ⓮ **Good City Brewing** offers a variety of craft beers brewed on site, a full menu, and tours of the brewing facility on Saturdays. The motto is "Seek the Good," and that's definitely the vibe in here. There is a second Good City location downtown, next to Fiserv Forum, the Milwaukee Bucks' new home.

⓯ **Koppa's Fulbeli Deli** looks like a run-of-the-mill corner grocery store, and it is, but it's also a spot to play 1980s Atari, take in the taxidermy art, and grab a Hodag (oh, the cranberry mustard!) or a Deli Lamma sandwich from the award-winning deli. Although Koppa's is no longer owned by the Koppa family, the spirit of the clan's sense of humor lives on between the aisles of this quirky food mart. Across the street, Comet Cafe offers scratch-made comfort food like meat loaf, stuffed pork chops, tuna-mac casserole, and a vegan Salisbury steak. The entrées are all fine and good, but the bacon mashed potatoes and gravy could be a life-changing food event.

A replica of the cabin where Milwaukee's first mayor, Solomon Juneau, lived.

And for classic, cracker-thin-crust Milwaukee pizza, the old-school ⓰ **Zaffiro's Pizza** is the place. As the sign will tell you, it's been around since 1954 and has managed to maintain the charm ever since—down to the last red check on the tablecloths. Take a right on Ogden Avenue and head back to the beginning of the walk.

The East Side

Points of Interest

1. County Clare 1234 N. Astor St., 414-272-5273, countyclare-inn.com
2. The Knickerbocker on the Lake 1028 E. Juneau Ave., 414-276-8500, knickerbockeronthelake.com
3. Jewish Museum Milwaukee 1360 N. Prospect Ave., 414-390-5730, jewishmuseummilwaukee.org
4. Wisconsin Conservatory of Music 1584 N. Prospect Ave., 414-276-5760, wcmusic.org
5. The Shorecrest (private residences) 1962 N. Prospect Ave.
6. Colectivo–Prospect 2211 N. Prospect Ave., 414-273-3753, colectivocoffee.com
7. Maryland Avenue Montessori School 2418 N. Maryland Ave., 414-906-4800, www5.milwaukee.k12.wi.us/school/maryland
8. The Jazz Estate 2423 N. Murray Ave., 414-964-9923, jazzestate.com
9. Paddy's Pub 2339 N. Murray Ave., 414-223-3496, paddyspub.net
10. Von Trier 2235 N. Farwell Ave., 414-272-1775, vontriers.com
11. Crossroads Collective 2238 N. Farwell Ave., 414-763-9081, crossroadscollectivemke.com
12. Oriental Theatre 2230 N. Farwell Ave., 414-276-5140, mkefilm.org/oriental-theatre
13. Ma Fischer's 2214 N. Farwell Ave., 414-271-7424, mafischers.com
14. Good City Brewing 2108 N. Farwell Ave., 414-539-4343, goodcitybrewing.com
15. Koppa's Fulbeli Deli 1940 N. Farwell Ave., 414-273-1273
16. Zaffiro's Pizza 1724 N. Farwell Ave., 414-289-8776, zaffirospizza.com

17 Riverwest's Center Street
Peace, Love, and Punk Rock

Above: Snail's Crossing, a community playground with sculptures designed and built by students from local elementary schools with guidance from artist Marina Lee

BOUNDARIES: E. Burleigh St., E. Clarke St., N. Humboldt Blvd., N. Booth St.
DISTANCE: Approximately 2 miles
DIFFICULTY: Easy
PARKING: Parking lot on Center and Booth Streets (read sign) or street parking
PUBLIC TRANSIT: MCTS route 15 (on Holton, 1 block west of the starting spot) and
Route 14 (Humboldt)

Center Street is one of the main thoroughfares in the Riverwest neighborhood, which received its name because it is located on the west bank of the Milwaukee River.

Riverwest hosts one of the most ethnically, economically, and culturally diverse communities in the city, featuring many unique bars, cafés, shops, and cooperative businesses. Riverwest has many festivals, including Locust Street Days and Center Street Daze. The neighborhood also features the Riverwest Art Walk, the state's largest walking tour of artists' homes and studios and neighborhood galleries.

Like Brady Street on Milwaukee's Lower East Side, Center Street underwent a revitalization process that started in the '90s and continues today.

Walk Description

Park near the popular nightclub and music venue ❶ **Mad Planet,** either on the street or in the lot on the southeast corner of East Center and North Booth Streets (be sure to check the sign at the entrance to the lot). Mad Planet is a Milwaukee institution that opened in 1990. The place is packed every Friday night for Retro Dance Party. It also hosts live music, including big names like Arcade Fire, The Black Keys, Black Lips, and Phox, as well as multitudes of local bands.

As you get your bearings, note ❷ **Cream City Hostel** across East Center Street at the northeast corner of its intersection with Holton Street. Milwaukee's first international hostel renovated a neoclassical-style building originally built for Holton Street State Bank. It's difficult to imagine now, but according to city records a permit was pulled in 1904 to move a barn from the site for the bank's construction. The hostel, which opened in 2019, offers affordable private or multibed rooms to travelers looking for an alternative to a hotel.

In his neighborhood history, Tom Tolan writes that Riverwest was once swaths of larger properties on the Milwaukee River held by wealthy German residents alongside patches of land where often-poorer Polish residents kept farm animals on their city plots. Among the bungalows in this densely populated area are many remaining Polish flats. As Polish families grew, they ran out of room in these houses built on narrow city lots so, rather than putting an addition on the side or back (where often another house, or alley cottage, already existed), many homes in the area were lifted and their foundations built up to create new "garden level" living quarters.

Walk east on East Center Street, one of Riverwest's commercial corridors, to ❸ **Company Brewing,** a brewpub and one of Milwaukee's few medium-size music venues. Take a right (south) at the brewery onto North Fratney Street, noting the slightly newer bungalow-style houses.

❹ **The Riverwest Co-op and Cafe,** a member-owned small grocery store and restaurant, is on the next corner along with the vintage ❺ **Falcon Bowl,** home of the fraternal organization Polish Falcons of America Nest 725, the last of its kind in Wisconsin. The basement bowling alley, built at the turn of the 20th century, features both an upstairs meeting space that is used for many neighborhood events and a classic Milwaukee bar with cheap beer on tap and a colorful history.

Take a left on East Clarke Street. At the end of the next block stands one of the neighborhood's many community gardens with the eclectic **6** **Bremen Cafe** just across North Bremen Street. Although it started out as only a café, Bremen Cafe is a bar with live music and comedy these days.

Turn left on Bremen and walk past **7** **Our Lady of Divine Providence** Catholic parish on the right, built in the 1890s as St. Casimir Church to accommodate the large number of Polish Catholic immigrants who formerly dominated this now diverse neighborhood.

Take a right (east) back on East Center Street, walk three blocks to the traffic light and cross North Humboldt Boulevard. As you do, note **8** **The Uptowner.** Affectionately and jokingly known as the city's Home of the Beautiful People, it's filled with day and night drinkers from all corners of the city and has a solid selection of pinball machines and a pool table.

Take a left on Humboldt after crossing at the light and walk north toward **9** **Gordon Park.** Its pavilion serves as a community hub and meeting place, and as a polling station. Consider walking around the park and exploring it a bit, not only for its natural beauty and community spirit but also for its hidden history. One leg on the 125-mile Oak Leaf Trail runs through the park, and at the park's southern end is a trailhead for the former railroad line The Beerline Trail, named for the freight trains that once hauled ingredients to Milwaukee's breweries. Heartier urban hikers might walk down one of the paths through the trees to the Milwaukee River, where what remains of the foundation for the Gordon Park Bath House can be seen in all its present-day graffitied glory.

The member-owned Riverwest Co-op and Cafe, located in a former Schlitz tied house (an establishment under contract to buy from Schlitz) dating to 1904

At East Locust Street cross Humboldt again, and take care to note ⑩ **Ma Baensch's** building on the southwest corner. Lina "Ma" Baensch and her two sons started selling pickled herring in 1932, during the Great Depression. Available packed in a fresh marinade or cream sauce, herring is usually eaten on crackers. In parts of Wisconsin, it is considered good luck to eat the cold white fish chunks on New Year's Eve.

Once you cross Humboldt, take a right to keep heading north up the boulevard away from Gordon Park. Smell something like burnt marshmallows as you head north? That would be coffee beans roasting at ⑪ **Colectivo,** a locally owned chain and popular citywide meeting spot. There are 13 Colectivo cafés in Milwaukee, 5 in Chicago, and 4 in Madison. This is Colectivo's main roasting facility. It was renovated from an old car dealership building in 2007.

Beginning on this block, travelers during summer and fall can enjoy the plantings in the boulevard along Humboldt, which extend north six blocks to Kern Park.

Cappuccino in hand, take a left at Colectivo on East Chambers Street. This unique little block is host to both the funky micro-size music venue Circle-A-Cafe and to Bliffert Hardware, one of the last independently owned and operated hardware stores in Milwaukee.

Take a right on North Bremen Street. If you didn't expend all your youthful energy at the playground in Gordon Park, then let your inner child run free in ⑫ **Snail's Crossing Playground.** The triangular piece of land was reclaimed by community resident activists in 2003 and adorned with ceramic installations designed and built by students from La Escuela Fratney and Riverwest Elementary School with guidance from local artist Marina Lee.

After nearly playing yourself out, save enough energy to turn left on East Burleigh Street at the northern tip of Snail's Crossing. In one block, turn left (south) at North Fratney Street. Proceed two blocks to East Locust Street.

To your left, one building west, is ⑬ **Woodland Pattern Book Center,** a nonprofit book shop that specializes in small-press literature. It's also an art gallery and performance space. Woodland Pattern opened in 1979 and hosts an annual fundraiser called The Poetry Marathon, a benefit for the organization that offers 15 hours of live poetry readings by approximately 150 writers.

Cross East Locust Street and take a left, heading one block east, back to North Bremen Street. After the cappuccino and all that playing around in Snail's Crossing, many people would be ready for a craft beer, readily available at ⑭ **Black Husky Brewing.** This dog-friendly brewery moved from a small log cabin in northern Wisconsin to urban Riverwest in 2016.

Feeling like a proper Milwaukeean now with beer froth fresh on your lips, head south on Bremen, back toward East Center Street. There will be another chance to wet your whistle after the two-block jaunt at ⑮ **Foundation,** a neighborhood hangout that's received worldwide attention

Fuel Cafe's original, grungier location opened in 1993.

for its impeccable tiki/Polynesian decor, including ranking fourth in Critiki's list of the 10 best tiki bars in the world. A creative mix of tropical tiki drinks tops the menu, but Foundation is also a welcoming place to stop in for a beer or three.

Take a right (west) on East Center Street. This block has a lot to offer, including ⑯ **Riverwest Film & Video**—a vintage video and film equipment rental store and home of Riverwest community radio station WXRW 104.1—and ⑰ **Fuel Cafe.** "The Fuel" opened in 1993 and was Milwaukee's first Seattle-inspired coffee shop. Stop in for "killer coffee [roasted by Colectivo] and lousy service." They also have stellar chili, burritos, and sandwiches. Try the house classic, the gooey, crusty Cheesy Tomato sandwich. There is a second Fuel on Fifth Street in Walker's Point (Walk 12, page 66), but this one is louder and grungier. Continue walking west on Center Street for a couple of blocks, back to the starting point.

Points of Interest

❶ **Mad Planet** 533 E. Center St., 414-263-4555, mad-planet.net

❷ **Cream City Hostel** 500 E. Center St., 414-510-2181, creamcityhostel.com

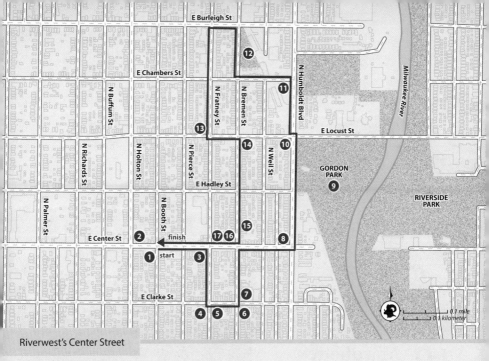

Riverwest's Center Street

3 **Company Brewing** 735 E. Center St., 414-930-0909, companybrewing.com

4 **Riverwest Co-op** 733 E. Clarke St., 414-264-7933, riverwestcoop.org

5 **Falcon Bowl** 801 E. Clarke St., 414-264-0680

6 **Bremen Cafe** 901 E. Clarke St., 414-431-1932, bremencafe.com

7 **Our Lady of Divine Providence** 2600 N. Bremen St., 414-264-0049, ourladyofdivineprovidence.org

8 **Uptowner** 1032 E. Center St., 414-368-0809, uptownerbar.com

9 **Gordon Park** 2828 N. Humboldt Blvd., 414-257-7275, countyparks.com

10 **Ma Baensch** 1025 E. Locust St., 414-562-4643, mabaensch.com

11 **Colectivo–Humboldt** 2999 N. Humboldt Blvd., 414-292-3320, colectivocoffee.com/cafes/humboldt

12 **Snail's Crossing** 3050 N. Bremen St.

13 **Woodland Pattern Book Center** 720 E. Locust St., 414-263-5001, woodlandpattern.org

14 **Black Husky Brewing** 909 E. Locust St., 414-509-8855, blackhuskybrewing.com

15 **Foundation** 2718 N. Bremen St., 414-374-2587, foundationbar.com

16 **Riverwest Film & Video** 824 E. Center St., 414-265-7420

17 **Fuel Cafe** 818 E. Center St., 414-374-3835, facebook.com/originalfuelcafe, fuelcafe.com

18 Marquette
A West Side Story

BOUNDARIES: W. Wells St., S. Emmber Ln., N. Eighth St., N. 27th St.
DISTANCE: 3.85 miles
DIFFICULTY: Easy
PARKING: Metered street parking near Eighth and Wells Sts.
PUBLIC TRANSIT: MCTS routes 12, 23, 30, and 31 and Gold and Blue Lines

The Marquette University campus adds a college town flavor to the distinctly urban neighborhood of Avenues West. The area was once home to bankers, beer barons, and other magnates, with far poorer, typically Irish Catholic residents down Tory Hill, on which the Marquette Interchange of I-94, I-794, and I-43 now sits.

The university slowly acquired new spaces in the neighborhood while adding academic programs over the years. In the mid-1960s, an urban renewal plan bolstered by the city finally aided in creating more of a closed-campus environment for Marquette, but, like other urban institutions of higher education, the university's boundary remains permeable, and it's this mix of academic, residential, commercial, and recreational spaces that gives Avenues West its special feel.

Today, numerous quintessential restaurants like Real Chili and Sobelmans have second locations in the neighborhood to accommodate Marquette students and west-downtown residents alike.

There are also many spots for a quick bite or cup of coffee. And with college students come music and beer—both of which are found on this route, including at the massive, storied Rave/Eagles Club and Third Space Brewery, one of the many small craft breweries that have opened in Milwaukee in the past decade. Brewing beer has always been synonymous with Milwaukee—hence its nickname Brew City—but whereas macrobreweries like Miller and Pabst once made most of the beer here, the scene now includes dozens of smaller breweries too.

Walk Description

Start on North Eighth Street opposite ❶ Centennial Hall, which was opened as a lecture hall in 1912 when the Milwaukee Public Museum shared space with the library. Renovations to the hall were completed in 1981, and it is now fully part of the Milwaukee Public Library. Walk north to the Wells Street intersection.

Founded in 1882, the ❷ Milwaukee Public Museum is a natural and human history museum housing more than 4 million specimens. Construction began on the current building in 1960; before moving here, the museum had shared space since 1898 with the public library across the street. *The Streets of Old Milwaukee* is one of the most popular exhibits, taking guests back to 1900s Milwaukee. The live tropical butterfly exhibit and the Costa Rican *Rainforest* are also visitor favorites. And anyone who visits the Milwaukee Public Museum must locate the famous Snake Buttons. Ask museum workers for more details.

Take a left (west) on West Wells Street. The grand ❸ Milwaukee County Courthouse is a neoclassical structure built in 1931 and now listed on the National Register of Historic Places. Architect Frank Lloyd Wright once called it a "million dollar rock pile."

Continue walking west on Wells Street. Once over the freeway, the campus of Marquette University spreads out ahead. Marquette is a Jesuit university founded in 1881 by the first bishop of Milwaukee, John Martin Henni, fully realizing Henni's mission to do so since arriving in Milwaukee in 1843, before it was a city and even before it had a high school. Today Marquette offers more than 80 majors. The Marquette Golden Eagles are a Division I member of the NCAA and compete in the Big East Conference. The ❹ Al McGuire Center, on the left, is among the first university buildings on the walk. It is named after the basketball coach who led Marquette to an NCAA championship.

A couple of blocks down on the left are ❺ **Sobelmans** and Real Chili (get a bowl with noodles!). These are second locations of iconic Milwaukee restaurants and, along with The Dogg Haus, are popular campus destinations for students and other city residents. The TV towers visible ahead belong to ❻ **WISN.** The ABC affiliate in Milwaukee, known as Channel 12, has been owned by the Hearst Corporation since 1955. Hearst changed the station to its current call letters, and subsequently built this location and moved its studio here in 1957.

❼ **Conway's Smokin' Bar & Grill** is a quirky Irish pub and restaurant that's been a Wells Street staple for more than 40 years. It started out as a one-room bar and over time spread out into three more adjoining storefront spaces. Originally just called Conway's, the *smokin'* part was added in 2004 when they began to smoke meats. Be sure to look for the stuffed monkey.

Take a left on North 27th Street, and enter the SoHi (South of Highland Avenue) neighborhood. ❽ **Daddy's Soul Food & Grille** offers a daily soul food buffet with a choice of meat that varies but usually includes ribs, fried chicken, baked chicken, meat loaf, pork chops, and tilapia, along with sides like macaroni and cheese, buttery greens, dressing, sweet potatoes, beans, rice, mashed potatoes, and cornbread muffins.

Turn left (east) on Wisconsin Avenue. ❾ **The Rave/Eagles Club** is a music venue featuring six stage areas, including the massive, oval-shaped Eagles Ballroom on the second floor. The Rave Hall is a smaller venue on the main floor. Built in 1927 for the Fraternal Order of Eagles, the Eagles Club once hosted big bands and was the focus of protests by the NAACP for the club's segregationist policies in the 1960s. Since the building reopened as a music venue in 1992, concertgoers as well as performers often try to find its swimming pool in the basement; although it does still exist, few have actually seen it.

The ❿ **Ambassador Hotel** is an Art Deco structure with marble floors, ornate plasterwork, and an upscale bar and restaurant. It is also known for being the location where serial killer Jeffrey Dahmer murdered his first victim. The floor on which this happened has been completely reconfigured, so the exact room no longer exists. The Irish Cultural and Heritage Center of Wisconsin, in the next block on the right, hosts Irish music concerts, cultural events, and more. Just before you reach 20th Street is the ⓫ **Pabst Mansion,** the former home of lake steamer captain turned brewing baron Captain Frederick Pabst and his family. It is open for tours and events.

Take a right (south) on North 16th Street. In 1894, The ⓬ **16th Street Viaduct** became Milwaukee's second viaduct. Beginning in the summer of 1967, Father James Groppi, a Roman Catholic priest and civil rights activist, led marchers seeking fair housing for African Americans across

Featuring multiple event venues, The Rave/Eagles Club was the focus of civil rights protests in the 1960s.

the viaduct, dubbed Milwaukee's Mason-Dixon Line. In 1988, the bridge was renamed the James E. Groppi Unity Bridge and is still occasionally a place of protest.

As you cross over Saint Paul Avenue on the bridge, notice to the right the original Sobelmans bar and just beyond it, BBC Lighting, an impressive yet quirky showroom with more than 500,000 decorative light fixtures for sale—and free popcorn! On the left, note Third Space Brewing, one of Milwaukee's many small craft breweries, owned and operated by lifelong Milwaukeeans.

After crossing above the Menomonee River, take a look at Marquette University's Valley Fields below on the right. These host games and practices for university soccer, lacrosse, and track and field. In winter, a dome placed over a portion of the field allows for continued use.

🔞 **Potawatomi Hotel & Casino,** owned and operated by the Forest County Potawatomi Community, first opened in 1991 and underwent major renovations in 2017 that included the addition of a second tower to the hotel. The casino is open 24/7 and offers slots, bingo, poker, blackjack, and other table games, plus off-track betting. Restaurant options range from the upscale Dream Dance Steakhouse to a sushi and Asian-fusion spot called RuYi to a massive buffet famous for its all-you-can-eat crab legs on Wednesday and Friday nights.

With the hotel and casino towering above you, go left off the viaduct on South Emmber Lane, which makes its way down to the valley below the bridge.

Emmber crosses the Menomonee River again, putting you much closer to the water this time, and ambles its way out of the valley, becoming North 13th Street, passing under I-94, and then dead-ending back at the Marquette campus. Cross West Tory Hill Street here and head onto campus. The **14 Haggerty Museum of Art,** opened in 1984, houses the university's art collection.

Visible behind the museum is the university law school, and ahead is the college of business. Go right on Wisconsin Avenue at Marquette Hall, a university landmark with a Gothic bell tower that sends music out to the campus community on Wednesday afternoons.

Founded in 1894, **15 Church of the Gesu** is a Catholic, Jesuit parish. Although close in proximity, it is not affiliated with Marquette University. Its French Gothic architecture was designed by Henry Koch, who also designed Milwaukee's city hall.

Cross over the I-43 freeway. **16 The Wisconsin Club's City Club** is located to the left. The Wisconsin Club is a membership-based business and social club that originated in 1895. Members dine; play golf, tennis, and pickleball; swim; and enjoy an array of activities in and on the grounds of the spectacular mansion featuring elaborate mahogany woodwork, stained glass, parquet flooring, and inlaid tile.

The **17 Milwaukee Public Library** is a neo-Renaissance-style limestone building that was built between 1893 and 1897. It's believed to be partially inspired by the Louvre. The interior features intricate tile work, marble stairways, and a breathtaking domed ceiling in the lobby. Today, the library stores more than 2.7 million books along with magazines, newspapers, records, cassettes, CDs, and videos, as well as more than 1.5 million government documents. Turn left on North Eighth Street to return to the start of the walk.

Points of Interest

1 Centennial Hall 733 N. Eighth St., 414-286-3000, mpl.org/hours_locations/centennial_hall.php

2 Milwaukee Public Museum 800 W. Wells St., 414-278-2728, mpm.edu

3 Milwaukee County Courthouse 901 N. Ninth St., 414-278-5362, county.milwaukee.gov/en/courts

Marquette

- ④ **Al McGuire Center** 770 N. 12th St., 414-288-4668, gomarquette.com/facilities/al-mcguire-center/1
- ⑤ **Sobelmans @ Marquette** 1601 W. Wells St., 414-933-1601, sobelmanspubandgrill.com
- ⑥ **WISN** 759 N. 19th St., 414-342-8812, wisn.com
- ⑦ **Conway's Smokin' Bar & Grill** 2127 W. Wells St., 414-344-1262, conways-smokin-bar-grill.business.site
- ⑧ **Daddy's Soul Food & Grille** 754 N. 27th St., 414-448-6165, daddysoulfoodgrille.com
- ⑨ **The Rave/Eagles Club** 2401 W Wisconsin Ave., 414-342-7283, therave.com
- ⑩ **Ambassador Hotel** 2308 W. Wisconsin Ave., 888-322-3326, ambassadorhotelmke.com
- ⑪ **Pabst Mansion** 2000 W. Wisconsin Ave., 414-931-0808, pabstmansion.com
- ⑫ **16th Street Viaduct/James E. Groppi Unity Bridge** 16th Street between Clybourn and Pierce Streets
- ⑬ **Potawatomi Hotel & Casino** 1721 W. Canal St., 800-729-7244, paysbig.com
- ⑭ **Haggerty Museum of Art** 1234 W. Tory Hill St., 414-288-1669, marquette.edu/haggerty
- ⑮ **Church of the Gesu** 1145 W. Wisconsin Ave., 414-288-7101, gesuparish.org
- ⑯ **The Wisconsin Club's City Club** 900 W. Wisconsin Ave., 414-271-7510, wisconsinclub.com
- ⑰ **Milwaukee Public Library** 814 W. Wisconsin Ave., 414-286-3000, mpl.org/hours_locations/central.php

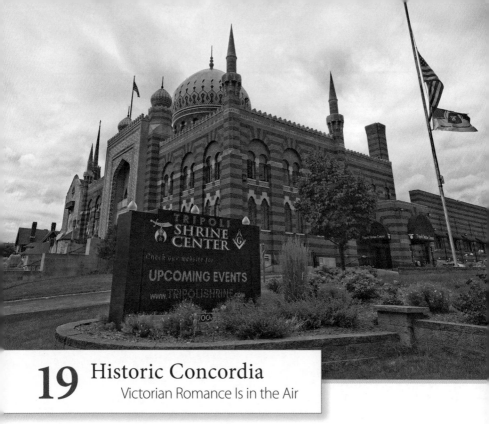

19 Historic Concordia
Victorian Romance Is in the Air

Above: With its massive 30-foot-diameter dome, the Tripoli Shrine Center is one of the best examples of Moorish Revival architecture in the United States.

BOUNDARIES: W. Juneau Ave., W. Wisconsin Ave., N. 21st St., N. 32nd St.
DISTANCE: 3 miles
DIFFICULTY: Easy
PARKING: Street parking on Wisconsin Ave.
PUBLIC TRANSIT: MCTS route 30 and Gold Line

The Concordia neighborhood features many Victorian homes that date back to the 1850s. At one time, there were scores more of these gorgeous dwellings in the area. Many of the remaining homes are spectacular mansions adorned with colorful paint schemes, stained glass windows, lush yards, castlelike turrets, and other now-rare architectural details. Every summer, the Historic Concordia Neighbors Inc. (HCNI) hosts one of Wisconsin's most popular home tours.

But the neighborhood offers much more than magnificent mansions, and for every free-standing home, there are multiple apartment buildings, which have been erected over the last 100 years as the neighborhood transitioned from a haven for the richest families in Milwaukee to a place where just about every demographic is represented. New developments, including restaurants and murals along 27th Street—Concordia's most commercial street—energized the area and started the nickname SoHi (South of Highland Avenue) for the eastern edge of the neighborhood. A strong network of spirited neighbors and organizations like Aurora Family Service, Penfield Children's Center, the Volunteer Center of Greater Milwaukee, and Neighborhood House contribute to the neighborhood's positive impact on the city, and coveted bed-and-breakfasts draw vacationers and staycationers alike.

The historic Concordia neighborhood is a microcosm of many parts of modern Milwaukee, a melting pot of people from different races and classes—as well as education levels—that range from temporary transplants to deeply rooted families and individuals.

Walk Description

Begin the route on the north side of West Wisconsin Avenue between 29th and 30th Streets. The ❶ **Tripoli Shrine Center,** Milwaukee's Taj Mahal–inspired Shriners temple built in 1928, was the first temple of the fraternal organization in Wisconsin, with 13,000 Shriners. The building is revered as an extraordinary example of Moorish Revival architecture in the United States; the style was also common for synagogues and movie theaters during the era. The massive dome is 30 feet in diameter, and two camel sculptures kneel at the entrance.

Walk west toward North 31st Street. On the corner, the ❷ **Brumder Mansion Bed & Breakfast,** one of several bed-and-breakfasts in the area, is a magnificent mansion built in 1910. George Brumder, a prominent Milwaukee business leader, built the home for his oldest son. The redbrick structure is designed in the English Arts & Crafts style, with elements of Gothic and Victorian. The B&B's five suites are named after the Brumders: George's Suite, Emma's Suite, Gwyneth's Suite, Marion's Suite, and The Gold Suite. What's unique about this B&B is its intimate, 55-seat Victorian-style theater that regularly hosts performances and events.

Take a right at the next block and walk north on North 32nd Street. At the next corner is the German Renaissance Revival–style Schuster Mansion Bed & Breakfast.

Take a right on Wells Street and cross to the north side of the street so you can get up next to the ❸ **Manderley Bed & Breakfast,** located inside an 1886 Queen Anne–style Victorian. Once home to David Howie, a rich coal merchant, and his wife, Adda, who was a published author and world-famous innovator in dairy farming techniques. For many years it was a rooming house that was almost demolished, but a couple purchased it in 1993 and spent seven years restoring the eight-bedroom home with four rentable rooms: Millie's Room, Bessie's Room, Franceska's Room, and Sophie's Room. Today, the couple's sons run the B&B, complete with a chicken coop—named the Taj Mahal—in the yard.

Take a left on North 29th Street and a right on West Kilbourn Avenue. These quiet streets feature more grand houses next to some modest yet adorable homes. Turn left on North 28th Street then left on West Richardson Place. On the left, ❹ **Neighborhood House of Milwaukee,** founded in 1945, has been in this location since 1967. It offers free social and educational services along with recreational activities for more than 4,000 people of all ages every year.

Turn left on North 29th Street, right on Kilbourn Avenue, and right on North 31st Street. On these blocks are some of the most remarkably kept old homes in this historic district.

At 31st and State, take a look down to the left toward the former Concordia College site, now the ❺ **Wgema Campus of the Forest County Potawatomi Community** and home to multiple renovated, multipurpose historic buildings, including a state-of-the-art data center.

Head right on West State Street. Look to the right in the middle of this block on State to check out ❻ **Dr. Robert Faries's home and observatory.** Built in the early 1850s, this is Concordia's oldest building. Faries, who was a dentist, was an astronomy enthusiast and built a telescope to view the stars.

Take a left on North 29th Street and walk two blocks north to cross West Highland Boulevard and enter the Cold Spring Park area. Cold Spring Park was once the site of horse races and the Wisconsin State Fair in the late 19th century. The area later filled in with more upscale housing.

Take a right (east) on West Juneau Avenue and walk through seven blocks of interesting mixed housing stock. The green space between North 23rd Street and North 22nd Street is the ❼ **Milwaukee Urban Tree House,** the 3-acre site of a U.S. Forest Service environmental education program. Across the street is Milwaukee High School of the Arts, a magnet school in the Milwaukee Public Schools system.

Turn right on North 21st Street. Spread over the next block to Highland Avenue is ❽ **Casa Maria** and three other houses operated in the tradition of the Catholic Worker Movement. Founded by Annette and Michael Cullen, Casa Maria has sheltered single mothers and their children, as well as entire families, refugees, and asylum seekers for more than 50 years.

Cross Highland Avenue and go another block south to West State Street. Take a right and go three blocks west. ❾ **Five O'Clock Steakhouse** is the oldest supper club in Milwaukee. Since 1946, it has undergone a few name changes but has never faltered in its ability to serve a perfectly cooked-to-order New York strip or filet mignon; handcrafted old-fashioned, Harvey Wallbanger, or Tom Collins; or—arguably the star of the supper club experience—predinner relish tray. Dimly lit and decked out in refreshed 1960s decor, the Five O'Clock is a step back in time and to this day is ranked as Milwaukee's favorite joint for high-end steaks and service.

Farther down State Street on the right is ⑩ **Mike's A Little Bit Country,** a day-drinking dive bar. The proprietor, Mike Christ, has owned five bars on State Street over the past 60 years. Other than country and Western tunes in the jukebox, there's little about Mike's that feels much like a country bar. Family and bar memorabilia, darts, and Brewers items are all that adorn the bar walls, along with stuffed animals lining the tops of mirrors, shelves, and the jukebox.

Turn left (south) on North 27th Street, into the SoHi commercial district. ⑪ **Daddy's Soul Food & Grille** offers a daily soul food buffet with a choice of meat that varies but usually includes ribs, fried chicken, baked chicken, meat loaf, pork chops, and tilapia, along with sides like macaroni and cheese, buttery greens, dressing, sweet potatoes, beans, rice, mashed potatoes, and cornbread muffins. The owner, Bernie Smith, is the head chef, and he or a family member created all the recipes. He named the restaurant after his father, also a chef, who passed away in 2014. Daddy's in SoHi is on the western edge of the Marquette walk (page 102).

Take a right on Wisconsin Avenue, past St. Paul's Lutheran Church, which was founded in 1841 and moved to the current location in 1917. Walk a short distance back to the beginning of the route.

The Manderley Bed & Breakfast offers the opportunity to stay in an authentic Queen Anne–style home.

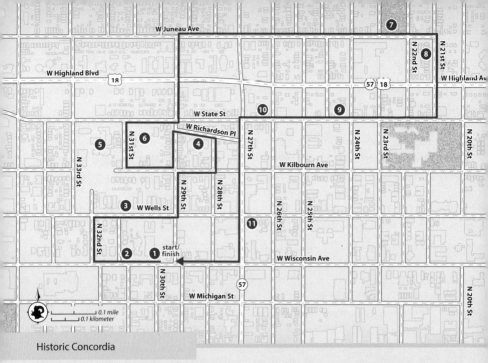

Points of Interest

1. **Tripoli Shrine Center** 3000 W. Wisconsin Ave., 414-933-4700, tripolishrinecenter.com

2. **Brumder Mansion Bed & Breakfast** 3046 W. Wisconsin Ave., 414-388-9104

3. **Manderley Bed & Breakfast** 3026 W. Wells St., 414-459-1886, bedandbreakfastmilwaukee.com

4. **Neighborhood House** 2819 W. Richardson Place, 414-933-6161, neighborhoodhousemke.org

5. **Wgema Campus of the Forest County Potawatomi Community** 3215 W. State St., Ste. 300; 414-290-9490; potawatomibdc.com

6. **Dr. Robert Faries's home and observatory** (private residence) 3011 W. State St.

7. **Milwaukee Urban Tree House** North 22nd Street between McKinley and Juneau Aves., tinyurl.com/urbantreehousemke

8. **Casa Maria** 1131 N. 21st St., 414-344-5745, casamariacatholicworker.weebly.com

9. **Five O'Clock Steakhouse** 2416 W. State St., 414-342-3553, fiveoclocksteakhouse.com

10. **Mike's A Little Bit Country** 2608 W. State St., 414-344-2716

11. **Daddy's Soul Food & Grille** 754 N. 27th St., 414-448-6165, daddysoulfoodgrille.com

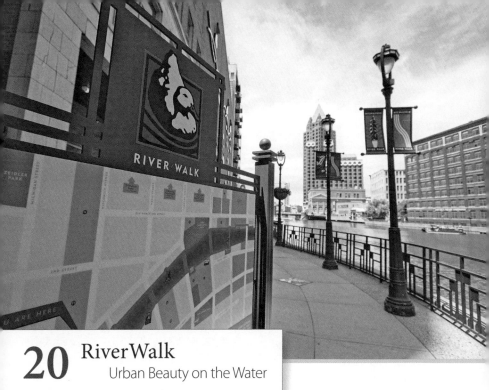

20 RiverWalk
Urban Beauty on the Water

Above: The RiverWalk extends 3.1 miles along both sides of the Milwaukee River.

BOUNDARIES: Pedestrian river bridge at Highland Ave., E. Clybourn St., Milwaukee River—
    east bank, Milwaukee River—west bank
DISTANCE: Approximately 1.5 miles
DIFFICULTY: Easy
PARKING: Pay lots, structures, metered street parking on Clybourn or Michigan St.
PUBLIC TRANSIT: West bank: MCTS routes 19, 23, and Blue Line; east bank: route 15 and Green Line

The Milwaukee RiverWalk is a commercial, residential, and recreational route along the historic Milwaukee River in the heart of the city that allows walkers to stop off at downtown restaurants, shops, bars, brewpubs, museums, and entertainment sites and to simply enjoy a revitalized waterfront.

Individual parts were constructed in the 1980s, and formal development began in 1993, but the RiverWalk had been an idea among city planners since the 1920s. The system is made possible through a Business Improvement District, a partnership between riverfront property owners and the City of Milwaukee. Property owners receive financial assistance from the city for any upgrades on their section of the path in exchange for public access.

The walk is adorned with permanent and rotating art pieces, including RiverSculpture!, an outdoor art gallery that features installations by national, regional, and local artists.

This walk focuses on the original, downtown stretch of Milwaukee's 3-mile RiverWalk, which also extends north along the west bank to Humboldt Avenue on the Beerline B and the Brady Street walk (page 54), and south along the east bank to the Third Ward walk (page 14).

Skyways are cherished during Milwaukee winters.

Walk Description

Enter the RiverWalk off East Clybourn Street on the west side of the Milwaukee River. ❶ **Milwaukee Boat Line** owns the double-decker *Vista King* and *Voyageur* tour boats that offer narrated history and architecture tours, happy hour sightseeing voyages (also known as booze cruises), concerts, dinners, brunches, and private charters.

Keep walking north along Riverwalk Way. The ❷ **Gimbel Brothers Department Store Building** is the block-length white structure at Wisconsin Avenue. The first Gimbels store opened in Milwaukee in 1887. According to Milwaukee writer and history buff Jeff Beutner, by 1925, the year this building was completed, Gimbels was the largest department store chain in the world. Gimbels achieved national fame from *Miracle on 34th Street* in 1947 and in the 1950s TV show *I Love Lucy*. The building also once housed a large Borders bookstore; today it contains a Planet Fitness, among corporate and business spaces.

Cross Wisconsin Avenue. ❸ **The Riverside Theater** is located in the 1928 Empire Building. While impossible to miss from the west with its

A maze of skyways connects downtown Milwaukee buildings.

new vertical sign hanging above its classic marquee, you can still catch glimpses of all this fabulous light from under and around the skywalk above you. The old vaudeville space was also a longtime movie theater and today is operated by The Pabst Theater Group, which also includes the historic Pabst Theater, Turner Hall Ballroom, and The Back Room @ Colectivo. The Riverside Theater hosts many national musicians, comedians, and other entertainers in its majestic setting featuring a Wurlitzer organ.

Also note the duck sculpture of *Black Bill* on the right. There are six duck sculptures on the RiverWalk, the most famous of which is *Gertie*, located on the railing of the Wisconsin Avenue Bridge. Gertie is the mother duck of *Black Bill, Dee Dee, Rosie, Freddie, Millie,* and *Pee Wee*. The statues were made in tribute to a real mother duck and her ducklings that nested in a precarious spot on the bridge in the spring of 1945 and became famous through reporting around the world—including a cover story by a reporter for *Life* magazine who wrote of them metaphorically as fragile but resilient survivors during the weary end of World War II. Overhead on the left, note the fish sculptures on the riverside wall of the Empire Building. Aptly named *Dream with the Fishes for Aurora,* the sculpture was created in 1998 by a San Francisco–based artist and updated in 2015 with LED technology.

Keep strolling on the west bank, past ❹ **Rock Bottom Restaurant & Brewery.** Opened in 1997, it's part of a 28-restaurant chain based in Broomfield, Colorado. All of the beer is brewed on site, and there are about a dozen different kinds on tap. The eclectic menu features steaks, tacos, a variety of mac and cheese dishes, pizza, burgers, and more.

Cross Wells Street and continue walking under the trellis. Enjoy the many different signs on the RiverWalk, such as the Usinger's sign visible from this stretch of the path.

Before crossing Kilbourn Avenue, note Milwaukee's Benihana restaurant because, like rapper Childish Gambino, we all "just want a quiet night down at Benihana." After crossing, the walk takes a slight left into ❺ **Pere Marquette Park,** a green space with a gazebo that features an outdoor concert series in the summer called River Rhythms.

At the park's north end, follow the walk left, then right and up to State Street. ❻ **Usinger's** is on this stretch. A 135-year-old German-style sausage business with 70 (!) varieties of sausage, it is still owned and operated by the fourth generation of the Usinger family.

❼ **Edelweiss Cruises and Boat Tours'** docks are located at Highland Avenue. Offering a variety of sightseeing, dining, and music tours, Edelweiss also has 10-passenger pontoons to rent so you can be your very own riverboat captain!

Had enough of the river? Here you can take a left down the short block to Old World Third Street to join the Brewery Neighborhood walk (page 8). For more riverfront action, cross over the river on the pedestrian bridge. Take a right off the bridge on the other side, following the paths back to North Riverwalk Way, and head south on the Milwaukee River's east bank.

Family-owned ❽ **Rojahn & Malaney Company** warehouse hugs the water here. Rojahn & Malaney Company is a third-generation wholesale floral distributor that's been around since 1929. It has been in its current location since 1954. The $1.4 million property has been for sale since 2016. That could buy a lot of carnations.

Riverwalk Way picks up again just to the left after crossing East State Street. Here you'll find the glass-fronted Bradley Pavilion, a 700-person riverfront event space at the ❾ **Marcus Performing Arts Center.** The Marcus Center opened in 1986 as the Performing Arts Center (longtime Milwaukeeans sometimes still refer to this structure as The PAC.) The name change came in 1994 when the Marcus Corporation donated $25 million for much-needed renovations and updates.

There are four major venues inside the Marcus Center: Uihlein Hall, the largest theater, is named after the Uihlein family, who owned the Joseph Schlitz Brewing Company (it always goes back to beer in Milwaukee). The three smaller theaters include Todd Wehr Theater, Wilson Theater at Vogel Hall, and the open-air ❿ **Peck Pavilion,** located on the Milwaukee River and adjacent to what was a grove of 50-year-old chestnut trees until the summer of 2019. The 20 mature trees were cut down to comply with a renovation plan, leaving Milwaukee divided on the issue.

The walk jogs to the right and then up to meet Kilbourn Avenue, where the Milwaukee Center office tower rises 28 stories above downtown. Completed in 1988, the redbrick building is part of a complex encompassing the block with a rotunda in its center and glass-ceilinged structures filling in the gaps between the buildings, which include the Saint Kate arts hotel and The Pabst Theater on the Water Street side of the block, and the ⑪ **Milwaukee Repertory Theater,** known as The Rep. Originally the Fred Miller Theater, The Rep's name change occurred in the 1950s. It has three theaters: the 205-seat Stiemke Studio; the 186-seat theater, bar, and

Usinger's sausage company, a 135-year-old Milwaukee institution

restaurant Stackner Cabaret; and the 720-seat Quadracci Powerhouse, which was originally the ⑫ **Oneida Street Station.** This building, located between the river and The Pabst Theater, was a power plant owned by Milwaukee Electric Railway and Light Company, the largest electric railway and electric utility system in Wisconsin. Its Milwaukee electric streetcar lines ran for 68 years, until 1958. In 2018, Milwaukee introduced its modern streetcar system called The Hop, which remains a controversial issue in now ostensibly car-centric Milwaukee.

Just across Wells Street and next to the China Gourmet restaurant stands the ⑬ *Bronze Fonz* statue—perhaps Milwaukee's most popular statue and certainly among its best selfie spots. Erected in 2008, the statue pays homage to Arthur "The Fonz" Fonzarelli, who was a lead character played by Henry Winkler in the Milwaukee-set sitcom *Happy Days*. The statue, like Winkler, is only 5 feet 6 inches tall and is forever giving the character's famous thumbs-up pose. In the summer months, public furniture is set out so fans can hang with the pop culture icon.

Take the steps down to the water, enjoying more public art, and stroll past the back of the City Center at 735 office building. Originally built in 1914, the 16-floor building is home to many businesses, including *OnMilwaukee,* a digital media company, online daily magazine, and city guide founded in 1998.

Cross Wisconsin Avenue. The Chase Tower is a 22-story high-rise whose tenants include Chase Bank and Milwaukee Public Radio (WUWM). WUWM has been Milwaukee's public radio station since 1971. It is owned and operated by the University of Wisconsin–Milwaukee.

Cross Michigan Avenue. The RiverWalk is a bit less exciting next to parking structures and with the I-794 freeway on the bridges ahead, but even here, the river water can be both invigorating and soothing.

Riverwalk Way splits here: to the right, it stays closer to the water and continues to its Historic Third Ward leg; to the left, it goes up a long ramp to Clybourn Street to the start of the walk. Maybe you want to hop on that booze cruise now after all this walking?

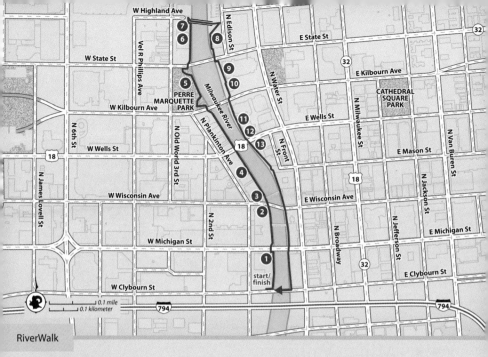

RiverWalk

Points of Interest

1. **The Milwaukee Boat Line** 101 W. Michigan Ave., 414-294-9450, mkeboat.com
2. **Gimbel Bros. Department Store Building** 101 W. Wisconsin Ave.
3. **The Riverside Theater** 116 W. Wisconsin Ave.; 414-286-3663 (purchase tickets), 414-286-3205 (box office); pabsttheater.org
4. **Rock Bottom Restaurant & Brewery** 740 N. Plankinton Ave., 414-276-3030, rockbottom.com
5. **Pere Marquette Park** 900 N. Plankinton Ave., 414-257-7275, countyparks.com
6. **Usinger's** 1030 N. Old World Third St., 414-276-9100, usinger.com
7. **Edelweiss Cruises and Boat Tours** 205 W. Highland Ave., Ste. 204; 414-276-7447; edelweissboats.com
8. **Rojahn & Malaney Company** 1005 N. Edison St., 414-276-7316, rojahnmalaney.com
9. **Marcus Performing Arts Center** 929 N. Water St., 414-273-7206, marcuscenter.org
10. **Peck Pavilion** 929 N. Water St.; 414-273-7121, ext. 216; marcuscenter.org
11. **Milwaukee Repertory Theater** 108 E. Wells St., 414-224-9490, milwaukeerep.com
12. **Oneida Street Station** North Riverwalk Way just north of Wells Street
13. *Bronze Fonz* statue North Riverwalk Way just south of Wells Street

21 Miller Valley
The Beer and the Bikers Go with the Flow

Above: The view as you drive into Miller Valley

BOUNDARIES: W. Juneau Ave., W. State St., N. 35th St., N. 46th St.
DISTANCE: About 1.5 miles
DIFFICULTY: Easy
PARKING: Street parking on W. Linden Pl., which parallels State St. from 35th St. to 37th St.
PUBLIC TRANSIT: MCTS routes 30 and 35 (on 35th St.)

It doesn't get more Milwaukee than Harley-Davidson motorcycles and Miller beer, and both have a huge influence in this neighborhood.

Miller Brewing Company was founded in 1855 by Frederick Miller after he emigrated from Hohenzollern, Germany, with his signature brewer's yeast. Today, this facility remains an active brewery with 800 employees who brew 8.5 million barrels of beer a year, including Miller Lite, Miller High Life, Miller Genuine Draft, Miller64, Leinenkugel's Summer Shandy, Coors Light, Blue

Moon seasonal brews, and Redd's Apple Ale. Corporate offices with more than 600 employees are also on site, as is a gift shop, a tasting room called the Miller Inn, and the spectacular Miller Caves.

The Harley-Davidson Juneau Avenue campus is also on this route. Although the location no longer assembles hogs (parts of the bikes were made here until the early 1980s), it remains the official birthplace of Harley-Davidson motorcycles. Today, the site employs 950 people in administration and marketing and serves as a magnet for moto fans who travel from around the world to visit, especially during one of Harley-Davidson's milestone anniversaries. The next big one will be the 120th anniversary in the summer of 2023.

Walk Description

With 35th Street at your back, walk west on West State Street, down into the heart of ❶ **Miller Valley,** forever considered the home of Miller Brewing. In 2008, Miller and Coors joined forces—technically it was SABMiller and Molson Coors—and in doing so combined 450 years of brewing heritage. As of 2016, the company is owned entirely by Molson Coors. MillerCoors moved its headquarters to Chicago in 2009, but today there are still roughly 1,400 employees working at this facility. The company has seven large breweries in the US; the three largest are in Chicago; Golden, Colorado; and Milwaukee.

Almost three blocks into the valley, a brick sign on the right announces that you've arrived. Parking lots and office buildings are partially obscured by trees. The curve in the road past North 38th Street is where the vista opens up.

The first thing that comes into view on the left is a replica of ❷ **Frederick Miller's Plank-Road Brewery.** A historical marker on the Miller Inn will tell you more about the Plank Road itself, but first note the entrance to the ❸ **Miller Caves** behind a fence to the right of the original brewery replica. The century-old caves are adjacent to the Miller Inn and just opened to the public in 2017. They were originally built during pre-refrigeration time to keep the beer at a cool and consistent temperature. Today the caves are one of the stops on the Miller Brewery Tour (brewery tours are a rite of passage in Milwaukee) as well as an occasional venue for concerts and other events. The first-ever concert in the caves took place in 2013, when actor and musician John C. Riley of *Step Brothers* and *Gangs of New York* performed with his bluegrass band.

Next door, the ❹ **Miller Inn** features old-world, Bavarian-style decor on both the first floor, in the Stein Inn, and on the second floor, in the High Life Room and the Champagne Room (remember, Miller High Life is the Champagne of Beers). Tourgoers get to sample a beer in the Stein Room and enjoy the stained glass windows, antique steins, and gorgeous woodwork.

Brewery tours are a rite of passage in Milwaukee.

The main production facility is the tall building across the street, and to get a peek inside you'll have to sign up for the tour. There are stairs—many, many stairs. You were warned.

Continue walking through the brewery complex, and note the signs on the buildings clearly stating what goes on, or what used to go on, inside. Just past North 41st Street, which leads to the modern shipping and receiving area, is a building with a sign reading STABLES above its second story. Unfortunately, there are no longer any horses to see if peering through the windows.

Cross under an enclosed pedestrian bridge. Brewery buildings on the right give way to more employee parking lots, and on the left is the ❺ **Miller Visitor Center,** home to the Girl in the Moon Brewery Shop, with a plethora of souvenirs and apparel. The shop is named after the famous advertising icon featuring a smiling young woman perched on a crescent moon. To this day, no one knows for certain who she is supposed to be (or who she was originally modeled after), but some believe it was the granddaughter of Frederick Miller.

Seventy-five-minute brewery tours are offered daily, about every 30 minutes from 10 a.m. to 3 p.m. The cost is $10 and includes beer samples at the beginning, middle, and end of the tour (with valid ID). Tourgoers also get a free Miller beer chip to use at one of 10 bars after the tour. Milwaukeeans will be the first to tell you that touring is thirsty work! There is, of course, also another bar in this area, a beer garden (weather permitting), and a 105-seat theater in which tours begin with a short history video.

Leave the MillerCoors campus—people know they're leaving because an arch over State Street marks the occasion and a slight wistful feeling overcomes them (that, or it's the beer)— and take a right on North 46th Street.

Turn right on Martin Drive, a serpentine, narrow boulevard with 1930s Cape Cods and Tudors. At the curve past North 44th Street, go to the low stone wall on the right for a view over the Miller Valley you just left.

At the top of the winding way, Martin meets West Juneau Avenue and curves sharply right. Beautiful, 1920s multistory stone apartments line the drive here, and Martin ends at West Highland Boulevard.

On the corner to the left is a 1927 building with a great garden area in front. **❻ 2Mesa Mexican Eatery** is the current concept to occupy this space—hopefully for the long term. The building formerly housed the venerated Highland Park Pies & Cafe and later Birdie's Cafe. 2Mesa is owned by esteemed chef Michael Feker, a passionate culinary artist and graduate of San Francisco's California Culinary Academy (CCA) who has worked around the world. 2Mesa is open for breakfast, lunch, and dinner. For something different, try the Mexican-style chicken schnitzel, a dish that pays homage to two of the largest ethnic groups in the city.

Take a right on Highland Boulevard. Two great views can be had on both sides of the boulevard: to the right, another look at Miller Brewing, and to the left, a long view of Highland Park and Harley-Davidson up the railroad tracks surrounded by dense woods.

Around the curve to the left is **❼ Highland Park,** a 3.5-acre Milwaukee County park that butts up against the Canadian Pacific Railway.

Highland Boulevard is nicely planted during the warmer months. On the right are the brewery buildings, which were partially obscured by trees when you first walked into Miller Valley, and on the left, through the trees, is **❽ The Harley-Davidson Motor Company's** Juneau Avenue headquarters. Better views of the compound are ahead at North 38th Street.

No longer a production site, the Juneau Avenue facility is the birthplace of Harley-Davidson, and hogs were cranked out here from 1903 to the early 1980s. According to an article by *OnMilwaukee* writer Bobby Tanzilo, more than 1 million bikes were made at this facility. Today, manufacturing and assembly work is done at Harley's Menomonee Falls plant; at a plant in York, Pennsylvania; in Kansas City; and in Tomahawk, Wisconsin.

This space is now used for customer service, marketing, a dealer-education site called H-D University, corporate office space, and meeting rooms. There's also a company store that sells

Juneau Avenue–branded clothing mostly to the employees, but it is occasionally open to the public during large Harley celebrations. The 100th anniversary of the company took place in 2003, and Milwaukee has hosted a massive H-D party every five years since then.

The 2003 event featured a concert that's a sore spot for many to this day. After months of hyping a secret headliner for the huge event, thousands of bikers were stunned and disappointed when Elton John took the stage. As quoted in an *OnMilwaukee* review of the show, "It would be a good show, but not tonight."

Milwaukee is also home to the Harley-Davidson Museum, which showcases more than 100 years of the company's motorcycles. It's a highly recommended Milwaukee must-do and is on the Walker's Point: Fifth Street walk (page 66).

Take a right on North 35th Street at Hope Lutheran Church to return to the starting point.

The Harley-Davidson Motor Company's headquarters, where bikes were made until the early 1980s

Miller Valley

Points of Interest

1. Miller Valley
2. Fredrick Miller's Plank-Road Brewery replica 3751 W. State St.
3. Miller Caves 3759 W. State St.
4. Miller Inn 3931 W. State St.
5. Miller Visitor Center 4251 W. State St.; 414-931-2337, 414-931-4280 (gift shop); millerbrewerytour.com
6. 2Mesa Mexican Eatery 4110 W. Martin Dr., 414-808-1594, 2mesa.com
7. Highland Park 4000 W. Highland Blvd., 414-257-7275, countyparks.com
8. The Harley-Davidson Motor Company 3700 W. Juneau Ave., 414-343-4056, harley-davidson.com

22 Vliet Street
Local Shops at Their Best

Above: Italian restaurant the Caradaro Club occupies a building that once housed a café.

BOUNDARIES: W. Vliet St., W. Martin Dr., N. 48th St., N. 60th St.
DISTANCE: Approximately 2 miles
DIFFICULTY: Easy
PARKING: Street parking on Vliet St.
PUBLIC TRANSIT: MCTS route 33

Vliet Street divides the neighborhoods of Washington Heights to the north, and Hawthorn Glen and Wick Field to the south. The Washington Heights neighborhood—particularly its Vliet Street commercial corridor—is one of the many Milwaukee neighborhoods to undergo a revitalization in the past decade. The other two neighborhoods are more sleepy, almost pastoral, despite being just across Vliet Street from this burgeoning action.

For most of the 20th century, Vliet Street was home to a heating-and-cooling company, a car dealership, and office buildings, but today it abounds with new retail owned by young, talented Milwaukeeans offering freshly roasted coffee, gluten-free pizza, glassblowing classes, and gelato.

These innovative start-ups mix well with longer-standing businesses like the iconic Times Cinema, the Caradaro Club pizzeria, and small but mighty Rainbow Booksellers. The area is also home to the Milwaukee Teachers' Education Association, home base for the educators who work in the largest school district in Wisconsin.

Walk Description

Start around North 48th Street and West Vliet Street with, perhaps, a cone from ❶ **Fred's Frozen Custard and Grill.** In Milwaukee, frozen custard—basically ice cream made with eggs—is preferred to regular ice cream. Although thicker and more dense than ice cream, custard is available in just as many, if not more, flavors. The Kopp's Frozen Custard chain is the most prominent purveyor of custard in the city. Fred's, which opened in 1967, also serves hot dogs and sausages, including a deep-fried hot dog called a Fred-Fried Dog. When the classic establishment went on the market in early 2019, dedicated customers were nervous about the change, but the new owners promised to "keep it Fred's."

Heading west, it's impossible to miss the building with the massive coffee cup on its roof. Not surprisingly, a café originally occupied the space, but it has been home to an Italian restaurant, the ❷ **Caradaro Club,** for almost a decade. Thanks to the popularity of cappuccino in Italian cuisine, the gargantuan roof cup still works. The Caradaro Club originally opened in downtown Milwaukee in 1945 as an Italian restaurant serving pasta and lasagna but soon added pizza to its menu, making it Milwaukee's first pizza parlor. Its crispy, cracker-thin crust, rectangular shape, and square slices inspired what is still the most popular style of pizza in Milwaukee to this day.

❸ **Dandy** is a good example of Vliet Street's revitalization. The vintage shop and event space, owned by a married millennial couple, is located in a former garage and is full of midcentury goodies like records, vases, lamps, furniture, and antique baubles.

Keep on trucking west and note the ❹ **Milwaukee Teachers' Education Association,** home of the union for the educators who work with Milwaukee Public Schools (MPS) students. Milwaukee has a strong public school system that serves roughly 80,000 students in 154 schools ranging in focus from arts to language to sports. Like all public school districts, MPS has its challenges, but it is also home to three of the state's and the nation's top high schools, according to *U.S. News*

& *World Report* and the *The Washington Post*. On a related note, in 1990 Milwaukee became a testing ground in school privatization efforts as the first community in the United States to offer a school voucher program. The program enables students to receive public funding to attend parochial and other private schools for free.

5 Wick Field, operated by MPS's recreation and community services department, is across the street. The neighborhood of the same name, located south of Vliet, consists of many hills and valleys, interesting streets, and very few people.

Keep strolling and consider popping into one of the many locally owned shops, galleries, and cafés on this stretch of Vliet. **6 Gietl Sign Co.** opened in 1982 to offer a range of signage, from digital to hand-lettered. **7 Square One Art Glass** is a full-service glassblowing "hot shop" and art gallery that offers classes, workshops, and finished pieces created by the shop's professional glassblowers.

On the next block, **8 Swoon** is a gift shop offering quirky, quality items—many of which are handmade—from clothing and jewelry by local, national, and international artists to original household items to fun trinkets and doodads. Swoon also offers workshops and classes. The woman-owned shop expanded to twice its size in 2019.

9 Rainbow Booksellers has been quietly selling books since 1981. The couple-owned shop is the last children's bookstore in the city, specializing in titles in the areas of science, math, culture, foreign languages, and art. They also have wooden toys, puzzles, party favors, and a candy counter.

10 The Times Cinema, built in 1935, has screened only independent, foreign, and American classic films for many years, but more recently has also featured mainstream films. It's also one of the few theaters to participate in the popular and prestigious Milwaukee Film Festival and is known for its Friday Night Freak Shows that showcase cult classics. Concessions include all the usual movie snacks and drinks, as well as thin-crust pizzas, appetizers like mozzarella sticks and waffle fries, and alcoholic beverages. They also serve Valentine coffee from next door. The Times is part of the Neighborhood Theater Group, which has two other historic theaters in the area: the Avalon Theater in the Bay View neighborhood and Rosebud Cinema in the suburb of Wauwatosa.

Next door is **11 Valentine.** Opened in 2009, the facility is both a coffee roastery and a café owned and operated by two Milwaukee natives. Valentine offers 10 regular coffees, including its signature Bering Sea blend with dark chocolate and hazelnut aromas. They also serve very select beer and wine, and coffee drinks spiked with bourbon, absinthe, vodka, grappa, and more. **12 Cold Spoons Gelato** is a locally owned shop that makes its cold stuff right on site, fresh every day. On Tuesdays, the mediums are priced as smalls, and the larges are sold for the price of a medium.

Take a left at North 60th Street, walk a long block to West McKinley Avenue, and take another left. To your right is ⓭ **Hawthorn Glen,** a 25-acre park and nature center also run by MPS's recreation department. It offers woods, a restored prairie, a playground, a duck-inhabited pond, picnic areas, a soccer pitch, and the Little Nature Museum, which is home to myriad living creatures. It primarily serves as an outdoor classroom, which according to the school district is visited by more than 12,000 MPS students every year.

Pass through the gate at North 58th Street, and take the path down into the glen. After a proper amount of nature exploration, climb back out to West McKinley Avenue and take a right.

Cross busy North Hawley Road and enter the Wick Field neighborhood again—welcome back. Take a right on Hawley and a left on West Martin Drive. This boulevard of striking homes and buildings extends up to Vliet, past Wick Field, but it has been blocked off and added to the parking for the school district's central services offices.

So take in what can still be enjoyed on the drive, and then hang a left on North 55th Street. Take a right back onto West McKinley Avenue. The Milwaukee Radio Group's broadcast station is tucked away in the trees here.

Take a left onto North 54th Street and a right on West Vliet Street, and walk six blocks back to the beginning of the walk.

Swoon gift shop expanded to twice its size in 2019.

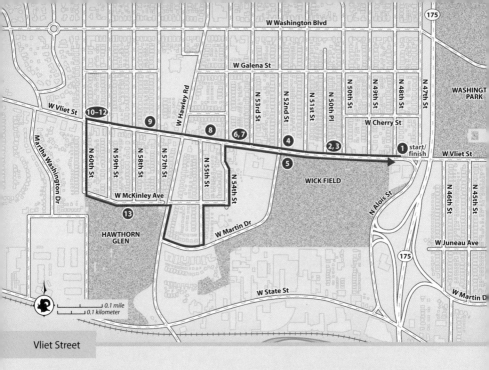

Points of Interest

1. Fred's Frozen Custard 4726 W. Vliet St., 414-771-6270, fredsfrozencustard.com

2. Caradaro Club 5010 W. Vliet St., 414-476-7700, caradaroclubpizza.com

3. Dandy 5020 W. Vliet St., 414-982-5020, livedandy.com

4. Milwaukee Teachers' Education Association 5130 W. Vliet St., 414-259-1990, mtea.weac.org

5. Wick Field 4929 W. Vliet St., 414-453-5057, milwaukeerecreation.net

6. Gietl Sign Co. 5300 W. Vliet St., 414-774-4690, gietlsign.com

7. Square One Art Glass 5322 W. Vliet St., 414-259-0811, squareoneartglass.com

8. Swoon 5422 W. Vliet St., 414-204-9579, swoonllc.com

9. Rainbow Booksellers 5704 W. Vliet St., 414-774-7205, rainbowbooksellers.com

10. The Times Cinema 5906 W. Vliet St., 414-763-1763, timescinema.com

11. Valentine 5918 W. Vliet St., 414-988-8018, valentinecoffeeco.com

12. Cold Spoons Gelato 5924 W. Vliet St., 414-727-9457, coldspoonsgelato.com

13. Hawthorn Glen 1130 N. 60th St., 414-416-0512, milwaukeerecreation.net/rec/Programs/Outdoor-Education/Hawthorn-Glen.htm

23 Sherman Park
Where Green Space Meets Gorgeous Architecture

Above: This 1924 Rustic-style home originally included a front yard pond.

BOUNDARIES: W. Roosevelt Dr., W. Lisbon Ave., W. Fond du Lac Ave., N. 51st St.
DISTANCE: 5 miles
DIFFICULTY: Easy
PARKING: Lot and street parking on N. 36th St. north of Fond du Lac Ave.
PUBLIC TRANSIT: MCTS route 23 and Blue Line are on Fond du Lac Ave.; route 60 runs on Burleigh

---

With 30,000-plus residents, Sherman Park is one of the largest neighborhoods in the city. In fact, it's so massive that it's subdivided into smaller sections, including Grasslyn Manor, Roosevelt Grove, Sunset Heights, St. Joseph's, and Uptown.

Primarily a residential neighborhood, Sherman Park is stocked with some of the city's most beautiful homes, many of which are elaborate, Tudor-style structures made from Lannon stone (a type of limestone found in Waukesha County) and brick. Many are located on larger-than-average city lots.

Sherman Boulevard showcases some of the most interesting and diverse architecture on the West Side.

For decades, European immigrants worked at nearby manufacturers such as A.O. Smith, once located east of 35th Street in what is now called Century City, which contributed to the prosperity of neighborhoods like Sherman Park and Rufus King to the north. From 1910 to 1997, more than 10,000 people worked for A.O. Smith, which became Tower Automotive in 1997 and then shuttered in 2006.

Six synagogues relocated to the neighborhood in the 1960s and '70s. In the late 1980s, one of the congregations, Beth Jehudah, founded the Yeshiva Elementary School and the Milwaukee Kollel, a center for adult education that attracted Orthodox families from all over the country to live within walking distance of the synagogue and its community.

Today, more than 200 Orthodox Jewish families live in the Sherman Park neighborhood. More than half of the Milwaukee-area Jewish population, however, lives in the northern suburbs collectively referred to as the North Shore.

African American residents started moving to the neighborhood in the 1960s to live near the factories where they could attain livable-wage jobs. But deindustrialization in the 1980s left many people unemployed, and the housing crisis in the early 2000s further adversely affected the people and businesses of the neighborhood.

In recent years, there has been an increase of folks of European heritage moving here, or moving back, for the historic homes and in search of a racially diverse, non-suburban environment.

As a neighborhood that has faced—and continues to face—economic and social justice challenges, Sherman Park is one of Milwaukee's most resilient communities, continuing to thrive and taking on all challenges.

Walk Description

Start on West Fond du Lac Avenue just south of North 36th Street. ❶ **Sherman Phoenix** is a four-level complex featuring 30-plus small, local businesses and a food hall with restaurants whose ownership is as diverse as their food offerings. In addition to wings, Southern-style desserts, spring rolls, ice cream, and vegan eats, businesses also offer beauty and wellness services and cultural activities. True to its name, the stunning Sherman Phoenix was literally built from the ashes of a bank that was damaged in a fire during the August 2016 Milwaukee Uprising, which attracted national attention after a Milwaukee police officer shot an unarmed black man, Sylville Smith, leading to multiple days of protests and riots.

Walk northwest on West Fond du Lac Avenue, crossing 36th Street. An eclectic stretch of sports bars, churches, insurance offices, and other businesses line this part of one of Milwaukee's longest roads. During the creation of the neighborhood, new zoning laws limited commercial property to specific streets and also account for the larger lot sizes. Sherman Park's homeowner numbers were devastated by foreclosures in the 2000s, so today many of the homes are being restored by new owners or are owned by mortgage companies and rented out.

Walk about 0.75 mile to the intersection with Roosevelt Drive. On the right, ❷ **Parklawn Assembly of God** is a large, interdenominational, multicultural church that proclaims, "We live in the real world . . . That's why we're focused on practical matters such as making faith work in family, career, and community issues." Its building also hosts a branch of the School of Urban Missions (SUM), a fully accredited Bible college and theological seminary based in El Dorado Hills, California.

Turn left on West Roosevelt Drive and right on West Keefe Avenue. On this little triangle of land sits ❸ **Sherman Perk Coffee Shop,** a café opened in 2001 in a former gas station by a married couple who still own and operate the business today. Sherman Perk, a play on the name of the neighborhood as well as a nod to the Central Perk coffee shop in the iconic sitcom *Friends,* also serves as a community gathering place where everyone, including pets, is welcome. The simple menu features coffee, tea, seasonal drinks, smoothies, bagels, breakfast sandwiches, and pizza. To accommodate the Orthodox Jewish population in the area, Sherman Perk serves numerous kosher beverages.

Across the street, ❹ **Milwaukee Kollel–Center for Jewish Studies** strives to build a strong and inspired Jewish community in Milwaukee. Thus its mission is to provide educational and experiential activities for local Jews of all ages.

Turn left (south) on North 50th Street, right on West Roosevelt Drive, and left again on North 51st Boulevard. ❺ **Congregation Beth Jehudah** started in 1927. Jewish services take place inside the modest building three times a day. The congregation also hosts social and outreach events on a regular basis.

Head though the campus and underneath part of ❻ **Ascension SE Wisconsin Hospital–St. Joseph Campus** (St. Joseph Hospital). It is the only hospital serving the near west side of Milwaukee. In the 1960s and '70s, St. Joe's was known as the baby hospital, and a seemingly endless number of Milwaukeeans now in their 40s and 50s were born there.

Walk six residential blocks (about 0.75 mile) to cross West Lisbon Avenue, which, like Fond du Lac, is a long commercial road that runs northwest out of downtown at an angle to the street grid. Here ❼ **Lisbon Storm, Screen & Door** has been in the business of selling, repairing, and installing windows, screens, and doors since 1962. They are known for their extensive inventory of parts, including salvaged antique glass, for old windows as well as new, and a knowledgeable staff.

The ❽ **French Immersion School** is a 40-year-old Milwaukee public school teaching students from K4 to fifth grade. The majority of instruction is in French, so English-speaking students learn to read, write, and speak in French. The Milwaukee Public Schools system also has a German Immersion School, an Italian Immersion School, a Spanish Immersion School, and a multilingual school called the Milwaukee School of Languages.

Turn left (east) on West North Avenue. On the right, ❾ **McBob's Pub and Grill** has provided Irish hospitality since 1986. The family-owned bar and restaurant is known for its corned beef sandwiches and Reuben rolls, but it also offers a coveted fish fry served with potato pancakes (considered by many Milwaukeeans, including this book's authors, to be the quintessential side to a fish fry). In a city often called out for its segregation, McBob's is a true melting pot. The clientele is a mix of neighborhood regulars and folks from all over the city who travel for the food, fresh Guinness, and "make yourself at home" vibe.

On the left, the massive Milwaukee Police Department 3rd District Communication Operations Center houses three municipal functions under one roof. The police station is located on the first floor; fire department administration inhabits the second floor; and emergency dispatchers work on the third floor. This corner once boasted the majestic Uptown Theatre, featuring an 1,800-seat auditorium, Art Deco chandeliers, and a stone fountain in its three-story lobby. In 1975, it made national news when a bomb scare abruptly stopped a Bruce Springsteen concert inside the theater. The Uptown closed in 1980 and was razed in 2001.

Turn right on West Lisbon Avenue and look across the street to the left. The no-frills **⑩ Judy's Red Hots** is an anchor on Lisbon Avenue, serving Vienna-beef hot dogs and Italian-beef sandwiches claimed by some as the best in the city. A popular spot during the day as well as at bar time, Judy's also serves gyros, burgers, hot wings, and fish dinners.

At the intersection with Sherman Boulevard, the **⑪ Washington Park Library** is a modern structure that opened in 2003. The bronze statue in front, commissioned by the Milwaukee Steuben Society in 1921, pays tribute to Baron Frederick von Steuben, a German soldier of the American Revolutionary War. Across the intersection is **⑫ Washington Park,** a 128-acre park that is home to the Urban Ecology Center–Washington Park. It also hosts weekly summer concerts called Washington Park Wednesdays and features a large lagoon where neighborhood children learn to fish.

Turn left (north) on North Sherman Boulevard. A handful of churches, big and small, along with Milwaukee Public Schools' Washington High School of Information Technology, break up the residences along the boulevard heading north to Sherman Park. The housing stock here is among the most interesting and diverse on the West Side.

Twenty-acre **⑬ Sherman Park** houses the Mary Ryan Boys & Girls Club. It also hosts a community garden, a project of the University of Wisconsin SEED Initiative. SEED stands for Sowing, Empowering, and Eliminating Food Deserts, just one part of larger state, county, and individual efforts to promote and support urban farming across the city.

Take a right on West Burleigh Street, with Sherman Park to your right. Turn left on West Fond du Lac Avenue to return to the start.

Sydney G. James's mural Steadily Rising *was commissioned for the Sherman Phoenix commercial complex, which was built on the site of a bank that burned down.*

Sherman Park

Points of Interest

1 Sherman Phoenix 3536 W. Fond du Lac Ave., 262-228-6021, shermanphoenix.com

2 Parklawn Assembly of God 3725 N. Sherman Blvd., 414-442-7411, parklawn.org

3 Sherman Perk Coffee Shop 4924 W. Roosevelt Dr., 414-875-7375, shermanperkcoffeeshop.com

4 Milwaukee Kollel–Center for Jewish Studies 5007 W. Keefe Ave., 414-447-7999, tinyurl.com
/milwaukeekollel

5 Congregation Beth Jehudah 3100 N. 52nd St., 414-442-5730, bethjehudah.org

6 Ascension SE Wisconsin Hospital–St. Joseph Campus 5000 W. Chambers St., 414-447-2000,
healthcare.ascension.org

7 Lisbon Storm, Screen & Door 5006 W. Lisbon Ave., 414-445-8899, lisbonstorm.com

8 French Immersion School 2360 N. 52nd St., 414-874-8400, www5.milwaukee.k12.wi.us/school/mfis

9 McBob's Pub and Grill 4919 W. North Ave., 414-871-5050, mcbobs.com

10 Judy's Red Hots 4812 W. Lisbon Ave., 414-447-7570, judysredhots.business.site

11 Washington Park Library 2121 N. Sherman Blvd., 414-286-3000, mpl.org/hours_locations
/washington_park.php

12 Washington Park 1859 N. 40th St., 414-257-7275, countyparks.com, washingtonparkneighbors.com

13 Sherman Park 3000 N. Sherman Blvd., 414-257-7275, countyparks.com

24 Mount Mary
Quintessentially West Side

Above: The Menomonee River Parkway offers a plethora of nearby trails.

BOUNDARIES: W. Burleigh St., W. Center St., N. 70th St., Menomonee River Pkwy.
DISTANCE: Approximately 5 miles
DIFFICULTY: Easy
PARKING: Park on the Menomonee River Pkwy. just south of Burleigh St., across from Mount Mary College.
PUBLIC TRANSIT: MCTS routes 60 and 28

This western part of the city has access to shopping and restaurants—primarily in neighboring areas like the next-door suburb of Wauwatosa—but for the most part it's quiet, family oriented, and inhabited by professionals.

The Enderis Park neighborhood—which part of this walk ventures into—is a particularly popular neighborhood among city workers and public school teachers. The neighborhood was named for a Milwaukee educator named Dorothy Enderis. A librarian and teacher, Enderis became the director of recreation in 1920 and created an award-winning recreational program that benefited many children and adults. She died in 1956.

There are also myriad small, family-owned businesses that thrive thanks to a supportive community, as well as lush green spaces. In short, this is a coveted, highly residential area that offers aspects of the suburban life inside the city.

Walk Description

Begin on the paved path along the beautiful Menomonee River Parkway heading south, with the river to your right. The lengthy parkway also continues to the north and into the next county with numerous trails running alongside. These trails range from under 1 mile to 29 miles in length and are a part of the Oak Leaf Trail.

On the left is ❶ **Mount Mary University,** a private, Catholic liberal arts university founded in 1913 by the School Sisters of Notre Dame. Mount Mary was Wisconsin's first four-year, degree-granting Catholic college for women. Today, the university has approximately 1,500 students and enrolls women at the undergraduate level and both men and women in the graduate school. Mount Mary has more than 30 majors and eight master's and doctoral degree programs.

Take a left on West Center Street. ❷ **Cashel Academy of Irish Dance** is the longest-running Irish dance school in Wisconsin. It was opened in 1982 by Marge and Dennis Dennehy and later taken over by their daughter, Kathy. The school has two other locations, in Madison and Kenosha.

Notre Dame Hall at Mount Mary University

Cashel Academy offers all levels of Irish dance to male and female students ages 4 and up, as well as regular public performances.

Next door is ❸ **Miss Molly's Cafe & Pastry Shop.** Molly Sullivan, a pastry chef who studied in France and Minneapolis, returned to Milwaukee and opened her dream business just a few blocks from where she grew up. The cute shop serves seasonal breakfast and lunch dishes and fresh bakery items, including cookies, muffins, scones, tarts, pies, and cakes. The café composts almost all waste and works directly with nearby farmers and businesses to keep a local flavor at this neighborhood sweet shop.

In today's world of big-box retail stores, it's refreshing to see that a place primarily selling lamp shades can still exist. ❹ **The Lamp Shade Shoppe,** across Center from Miss Molly's, also sells lamps and lamp hardware and has been around since 1970. This quiet corner store is particularly useful when looking for a new shade for a vintage lamp.

Cross North 92nd Street and take a left (on 92nd). Walk two blocks and then turn right on West Locust Street. After four blocks of mid-20th-century ranches and Cape Cods stands 8.4-acre ❺ **Cooper Park,** located in the heart of Milwaukee's historic Cooper Park neighborhood. The park hosts many events, including summertime movies, cookouts, and other social events year-round. The neighborhood is quiet, family oriented, dog friendly, and home to primarily professionals.

Keep walking east on Locust 1 mile to North 72nd Street. At North 76th Street, the neighborhood becomes Enderis Park. Similar in vibe and demographic to Cooper Park, Enderis Park also has nice-size city lots with Cape Cods, Colonials, and some Lannon stone bungalows. Turn right on North 72nd Street. ❻ **Enderis Park** has playfields on the north end and hosts community events, including a farmers market in the summer months and Concerts on the Green, a popular music series featuring local bands such as 5 Card Studs and Trapper Schoepp.

As the park comes to a point with West Locust Street at its south end, 72nd Street angles sharply right. Take a left on Locust. Just past the park, take a left on North 70th Street. The street curves slightly right as it meets West Lisbon Avenue, a long commercial corridor that runs diagonally northwest across the street grid from nearer the city's center. Take a left on Lisbon, noting across the street the Mother of Good Counsel, a Catholic church and a school that's been around for more than 80 years.

It's a short block to the next intersection, with West Burleigh Street. Spreading east and north for 85 acres from the northeast corner is Lincoln Memorial Cemetery, which was founded in 1894 as Wanderers Rest Cemetery by German Lutherans.

Take a left on Burleigh Street. ❼ **Gard's** is a family-owned corner tavern with a unique triangular bar. It has served the neighborhood since the 1940s. It's also known for its homemade clam

Family-owned Gard's has served the neighborhood since the 1940s.

chowder and offers, among other eats, a traditional Wisconsin Friday fish fry, Wednesday wing night, and Taco Thursday.

Travel west on Burleigh along an eight-block commercial corridor, past hair salons, insurance agencies, a vet clinic, gas stations, dentist offices, and the Raasch Raetz Funeral Home. Midtown Pharmacy 2 is one of three in a small chain of independently owned pharmacies, along with the predictably named Midtown Pharmacy 1 and Midtown Pharmacy 3.

On the left, past North 78th Street, note old-school **8 Happy Hobby.** In operation for more than 40 years, it's one of Milwaukee's last nonchain hobby stores with craft and dollhouse supplies. Across the street, **9 Collector's Edge Comics** is a Wisconsin chain with a large selection of comic books and graphic novels. They have a second location in the Bay View neighborhood on Milwaukee's south side. Many of Milwaukee's comics shops have closed in the past decade or two. Other survivors include Lost World of Wonders, The Turning Page, Vortex Comics, and several used book stores that carry comics, like Downtown Books.

Walk another five blocks past ranch-style homes and long rows of Cape Cods, all built between 1941 and 1954. The **10 Milwaukee School of Languages,** a public school serving grades 6–12, fills the next two blocks on the right. The three main languages studied and spoken are Spanish, German, and French. Students can also take Japanese and Mandarin Chinese. The Milwaukee Public Schools district has several language schools, including immersion schools in Spanish, French, German, and Italian.

A few more blocks of bungalows and two-story multifamily housing gets you to **11 Bunzel's Old-Fashioned Meat Market & Catering,** owned by a family who have kept their old-fashioned meat market thriving for four generations. Bunzel's offers a wide selection of farm-raised meat, from ground beef to brisket to oxtails. They also make their own sausages, and the deli offers sandwiches and dinners like barbecue pulled pork, baked ham, and homemade bratwursts. Bratwursts—or brats (pronounced brahts), as they are often called by Milwaukeeans—are German sausages of beef, veal, or, more often, pork. Brats are as popular as hot dogs when it comes to grill favorites and are usually topped with sauerkraut and mustard.

Walk along the northern edge of Mount Mary University's campus to return to Menomonee River Parkway and the starting point.

Points of Interest

1. **Mount Mary University** 2900 Menomonee River Pkwy., 414-930-3000, mtmary.edu

2. **Cashel Academy of Irish Dance** 9205 W. Center St., 414-773-9133, cashelacademy.com

3. **Miss Molly's Cafe & Pastry Shop** 9201 W. Center St., 414-249-5665, missmollyscafe.com

4. **The Lamp Shade Shoppe** 9202 W. Center St., 414-476-8020, lampshadeshoppe.com

5. **Cooper Park** 8701 W. Chambers St.; 414-353-3212; countyparks.com, friendsofcooperpark.com

6. **Enderis Park** 2956 N. 72nd St., 414-773-9948, enderispark.org

7. **Gard's** 7170 W. Burleigh St., 414-442-4280

8. **Happy Hobby** 7821 W. Burleigh St., 414-461-6013, happyhobby.com

9. **Collector's Edge Comics** 7826 W. Burleigh St., 414-445-5055, collectorsedgecomics.com

10. **Milwaukee School of Languages** 8400 W. Burleigh St., 414-393-5700, www5.milwaukee.k12.wi.us/school/msl

11. **Bunzel's Old-Fashioned Meat Market & Catering** 9015 W. Burleigh St., 414-873-7960, bunzels.com

25 Northridge Lakes
Nature's Beauty and Urban Decay

Above: The quiet Northridge Lakes neighborhood is centered around Northridge Lake.

BOUNDARIES: W. Glenbrook Rd., W. Brown Deer Rd., N. 70th St., N. 85th St.
DISTANCE: Approximately 4 miles
DIFFICULTY: Easy
PARKING: Park on 70th St. north of Brown Deer Rd.
PUBLIC TRANSIT: MCTS route 76

Northridge Lakes was once in Granville, a township and agricultural community that was annexed by Milwaukee in the 1950s under a municipal growth campaign by the city's third Socialist mayor, Frank Zeidler.

The neighborhood, and the Northridge Mall that opened in 1972 on the west side of Northridge Lakes, were both developed by the Kohl's corporation. Northridge Mall was the crown jewel of the neighborhood and one of Milwaukee's most successful malls from the

1970s to the 1990s. The mall closed in 2003 and, despite multiple attempts to revitalize the space, it remains vacant.

Strip malls partially occupied by chain restaurants and local businesses still line Brown Deer Road, but tucked away is Northridge Lakes, a hilly neighborhood with an abundance of green space and wide, curvy streets winding around Northridge Lake. Most of the northern part of the neighborhood remains undeveloped and partially wooded.

Walk Description

From West Brown Deer Road, head north on North 70th Street, a winding lane that travels leisurely along Northridge Lake, with multiunit apartment homes and condos often set way back from the street.

A planned community 50 years ago, ❶ Northridge Lakes and its commercial neighbor, the former shopping mall also with the Northridge name, were a vision of the Kohl's corporation, specifically Sidney and Allen Kohl, brothers of US senator Herb Kohl of Wisconsin. According to John Gurda in *The Making of Milwaukee,* original plans were "for 20,000 people, three artificial lakes, schools, a library, and assorted places of worship." It didn't turn out quite that grand, but the variety of housing is, and so is the setting.

About 4,000 people now live around the lake and west to about North 85th Street. The suburb of Brown Deer, which borders Northridge Lakes at roughly North 68th Street, adds another 12,000 residents to the area. Heading farther up North 70th Street, the quiet becomes palpable; it's easy to forget that this is part of Milwaukee.

Turn left on West Glenbrook Road, which goes around the north end of the lake. From this vantage, a bridge over the water can be seen across a field between the street and the water. Glenbrook naturally becomes North 75th Street; continue to follow that around the east side of Northridge Lake. A road on the left goes out to the Harbor Pointe apartments offices, which are on an island in the lake.

Continue south and take a right on Northridge Lakes Boulevard, crossing North 76th Street at the light. 76th Street is also WI 181, a major north–south corridor through the city.

The environment begins to fill in with commercial buildings as you approach the former mall. Take a right on Northridge Mall Road, which winds around the abandoned, fenced-off property.

❷ Northridge Mall had its grand opening in August 1972, two years after its sister mall, Southridge, opened in Greenfield, a suburb on the opposite end of Milwaukee. The big anchor stores, Boston Store, Gimbels, and Sears, were joined by a number of smaller stores that made a cultural impact on area shoppers. It's hard to overstate the significance of the mall to at least a generation of Milwaukeeans. Farrell's Ice Cream Parlour was the local Disneyland—if you were a Milwaukee kid in the '70s, it was the place to celebrate a birthday, feast on sweets, and escape the adult world for a couple of hours. The wholesome eateries—there was another in Southridge Mall—were re-creations of old-fashioned ice-cream shops from the 1890s. The memorable atmosphere included Tiffany-style lamps, a player piano, red flocked wallpaper, black booths, menus that looked like old newspapers, a vintage candy shop in the front of the restaurant, and employees dressed in barbershop quartet clothing. Farrell's was also known for its massive birthday sundae, which employees wildly brought out on a stretcher while ambulance sirens blared over the sound system. In 2004, a longtime fan of Farrell's tried to revive the concept when he opened Baker's Ice Cream Parlour & Eatery on Milwaukee's South Side. Unfortunately, the old-timey family restaurant didn't last long. Some things just can't be re-created

Looking at Northridge now, with grasses growing up between cracks in the parking lots as part of nature's slow reclamation, the empty buildings could just as easily be any empty commercial space, or just a warehouse—a place the 21st century forgot. Inside, however, Northridge is clean and well lit by spacious skylights, according to Andy Tarnoff in an *OnMilwaukee* article. After a private access tour, he wrote that the trees that were planted in the ground inside continue to grow and that some of the spaces are remarkably preserved.

Take a right to continue on Northridge Mall Road. The road that would otherwise continue to follow the perimeter of this old shopping mecca has been closed off for many years.

The mall road loops northeast past ❸ **Alexian Village,** a 60-acre not-for-profit senior living community that is open to all faiths.

Continue to North 76th Street and take a left (north). On the left, ❹ **Temple Menorah** is a diverse Jewish synagogue with the tagline "A synagogue where everyone knows your name" that is derived from the 1980s sitcom *Cheers.*

Turn left on West Glenbrook Road. The area to the right is largely made up of Kohl Park, with County Line Road and Milwaukee's city limits behind it. To the left is an interesting row of town houses that extends for a block. Glenbrook gradually curves, first to the left, then to the right, with late-20th-century Colonial-style homes along the right side.

Turn left (south) on North Burbank Avenue, left on West Fairy Chasm Road, and then right on West Northridge Lakes Court, which quickly becomes North 85th Street after five two-story apartment homes and a gradual curve to the left.

North 85th Street heads due south past more rows of low-set apartment buildings and slowly becomes more commercial. The nearly empty strip malls at times seem like peaceful aspects of a

Since closing in 2003, Northridge Mall has remained vacant.

natural environment instead of a built one, but with another glance they return to the reminders of capital flight and the ever-changing retail and cultural environment of the early 21st century.

Turn left (east) on West Brown Deer Road. Interestingly, ❺ **Menards,** the large home-improvement store that fills most of the view on the corner, is built on part of the parking lots adjacent to Northridge Mall and is reportedly doing quite well and may even expand. Menards is a family-owned company that started in 1958 in Eau Claire, Wisconsin, with stores now located across 14 states. Its success seems to run counter to the current anti-brick-and-mortar logic of the online-retail era.

Fast-food chains, a Salvation Army store, and cell phone and dollar stores line the smaller spaces along this commercial corridor, while the larger structures farther back from the street grow more and more empty.

❻ **ETE Reman,** however, disrupts this scene by occupying a former large Walmart retail space on the south side of Brown Deer Road. This remanufacturer of automotive transmissions was founded in 1985, employs 600 people, and moved most of its operations to this site from others around the city. Behind ETE Reman is the Servite Woods neighborhood. About 1,200 people live in this quiet corner of the city in low-rise multifamily dwellings.

Cross the busy North 76th Street intersection of traffic ramps. ❼ **Hmong American Peace Academy's Happy Hill campus** is a public charter school for kindergarten through second grade. HAPA serves over 950 Hmong American children across three schools in Milwaukee. Walk back to the start of the walk at North 70th Street.

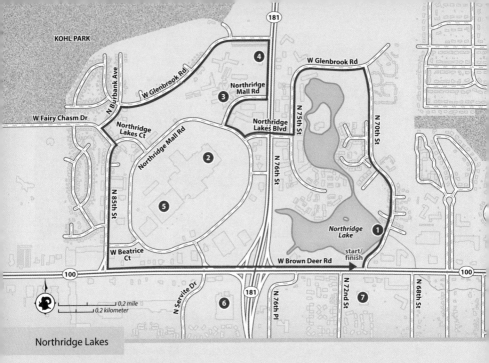

Points of Interest

1 **Northridge Lakes** (private residences)

2 **Northridge Mall** (permanently closed; historic site) 8110 W. Brown Deer Road

3 **Alexian Village** 9301 N. 76th St., 414-355-9300, ascensionliving.org/find-a-community /alexian-village-milwaukee-wi

4 **Temple Menorah** 9363 N. 76th St., 414-355-1120, templemenorah.com

5 **Menards** 8110 W. Brown Deer Road, 414-355-5666, menards.com

6 **ETE Reman** 8700 N. Servite Drive, 800-934-9479, etereman.com

7 **Hmong American Peace Academy's Happy Hill campus** 7171 W. Brown Deer Road, 414-797-0746, myhapa.org

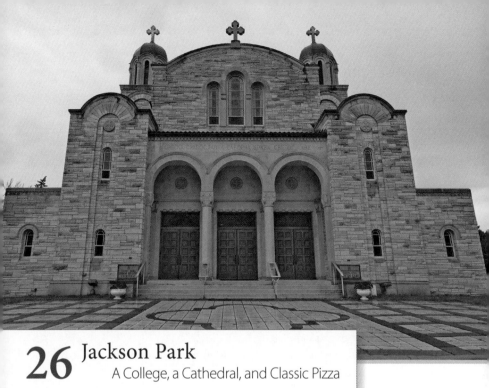

26 Jackson Park
A College, a Cathedral, and Classic Pizza

Above: St. Sava Serbian Orthodox Cathedral

BOUNDARIES: W. Kinnickinnic River Pkwy., W. Morgan Ave., S. 35th St., S. 51st St.
DISTANCE: 4.5 miles
DIFFICULTY: Easy
PARKING: In Jackson Park along Kinnickinnic River Pkwy.
PUBLIC TRANSIT: MCTS route 14

Milwaukee's Jackson Park neighborhood, named after President Andrew Jackson, offers a mix of amenities that includes popular restaurants, quiet streets, and a committed community. Jackson Park, the largest park on the South Side, and the neighborhood's proximity to the Kinnickinnic River give it easy access to nature. Alverno College is the heart of the neighborhood.

The Kinnickinnic River Parkway—and its lagoon—was created in the 1930s and into the 1940s. After this, the neighborhood experienced a boom in growth and population during the middle of the century, and the area remains a stable, coveted city neighborhood today.

Walk Description

Begin on West Kinnickinnic Parkway near West Forest Home Avenue. Walk west alternately on the paved path and the parkway around the pond at ❶ **Jackson Park** on your left. Note the two islands in the pond. To your right, out of sight but not necessarily out of earshot, railroad lines create an abrupt border at the park's north end.

The parkway exits Jackson Park at South 43rd Street. Take a left (south). In two blocks, take a right on West Dakota Street. In less than half a mile, Manitoba Park interrupts the rows of mid-20th-century Cape Cods and ranch-style houses. At 3.6 acres, Manitoba Park is one of the smaller Milwaukee County parks. Go another block of ranch houses with nice-size city lots, and then take a left on South 51st Street.

On one side of the intersection with Oklahoma Avenue is ❷ **El Rey Family Market,** part of a chain of Latino grocery stores on Milwaukee's South Side. This location was built in 2011 and features a Taco Loco sit-down cantina. There are four El Rey locations, with the largest located on Cesar E. Chavez Drive, at the westernmost end of the Walker's Point neighborhood. In 2019, one of the original founders, Armando Villarreal, passed away. He opened the first El Rey with his brothers, Ernesto and Heriberto, in 1978.

Family Music Center, across the street, is a musical instrument store that opened in 1994. It offers rentals, sales, repairs, and lessons.

It's impossible not to notice ❸ **Discount Liquor**'s sign across Oklahoma Avenue, which has become as iconic as the business itself. Family owned since 1960, Discount Liquor is a 4,000-square-foot emporium of local, national, and international libations. For better or for worse, consuming alcoholic beverages is deeply ingrained in Wisconsin culture; thus, Discount Liquor is always bustling. There is a second location in Waukesha, a town west of Milwaukee.

Walk through the intersection with Oklahoma Avenue. On the right, ❹ **American Serb Hall**—known simply as Serb Hall—is a banquet and wedding facility that opened in 1950 as a social place for the Serbian community. Today, it is well known for its Friday Fish Fry. Fish fries are a weekly Milwaukee tradition, particularly during, but not confined to, Lent. Serb Hall is one of the most famous, serving approximately 2,000 pounds of fish every Friday inside and from its unique drive-through and carryout window. Serb Hall offers breaded and deep-fried fish, which is the classic and some believe only way to consume fish on a Friday in Wisconsin, but they also have baked and Serbian-style fish, which comes slathered in a red sauce with peppers. Other than fish, there is one entrée on the Friday menu: a meat loaf dinner. If consuming alcohol with a fish fry, beer or the brandy old-fashioned (sweet or sour) are the Milwaukeean's drink of choice.

A lot of people like to eat at "suppertime," which is 5 or 5:30 p.m., so go later to avoid crowds, particularly during Lent.

Farther down the block is **⑤ St. Sava Serbian Orthodox Cathedral,** built in 1956 and adorned with traditional wall mosaics known as some of the most elaborate, extensive church mosaics in the United States. It's estimated there are about 5,500 Serbs living in Milwaukee today. Every summer for the past 65 years or so, St. Sava hosts a festival called St. Sava Serbian Days. The event attracts many non-Serbians in search of the delicious homemade food like barbecue lamb and pig, cevapi (sausages), sarma (stuffed cabbage), burek (savory pastry), and many sweets.

Milwaukee is known as the City of Festivals and has about 10 ethnic festivals every summer and fall. Many take place at the Henry Maier Festival Park, home of Summerfest, including Festa Italiana, German Fest, Irish Fest, Black Arts Fest, Polish Fest, and Fiesta Mexicana, but Milwaukee has myriad other church and neighborhood festivals that enrich communities across the city.

Cross West Forest Home Avenue and take a left (northeast) on Forest Home. Anyone who appreciates family businesses, thin-crust pizzas, excessive holiday decorations, vintage signs, and paint-by-number art collections will thoroughly enjoy **⑥ Maria's Pizza.** Maria Traxel opened the first location in 1957 and this location, the second, in 1971. Today, her daughter, Bonnie Crivello, co-owns the restaurant and works regularly as a server. The pizzas come in two sizes: a 14-inch circle or an 18-inch rectangle. Toppings are simple and include sausage, pepperoni, onions, mushrooms, black olives, and green peppers. The pizzas are served on baking sheets, and the edges of the pizza hang over the sides. Maria's does not have a liquor license, but they serve pitchers of soda, most famously the "blue soda."

The city of Milwaukee often has a most peculiarly shaped western boundary. Here, a pocket of the suburb of Greenfield is just to the south.

Alverno College, a four-year Roman Catholic liberal arts college, offers programs in business, education, nursing, and the arts.

Keep walking past the ❼ **Brass Key Restaurant & Lounge,** across on the left. This Greek, American, and Italian restaurant serves breakfast, lunch, and dinner and is the place for entrée variety and large portions. Brass Key also has a full, retro bar.

On the right on the next block is ❽ **George Webb,** part of a classic chain of Wisconsin diners founded in 1948 and known for giving away free burgers when the Brewers win 12 games in a row (it has happened twice in history) and for having two identical clocks on the walls. The clocks were the result of a Milwaukee ordinance and the founder's sense of humor: against a prohibition on 24-hour establishments, Webb declared that his restaurants were open "23 hours, 59 minutes, and 59 seconds, seven days a week and on Sundays." The two clocks were set one minute apart to demonstrate the opening and closing times.

Over to the left again, ❾ **Di Stefano's Pizza Palace** is a classic pizza joint that has been family operated since it opened in 1972. Pizza options include an extra-large pie with extra everything on it called The Godfather, and an olive-lovers pizza called The Olive Tree. Subs, salads, and pasta dishes are also on the menu.

A row of hair salons, insurance offices, fast food, and bars—including the uniquely situated Una Cafe, named for the river that flows through Croatia and Bosnia and Herzegovina—brings you back to Oklahoma Avenue again. Take a right and almost immediately another right (south) on South 43rd Street.

It's a block to West Euclid Avenue and just beyond a row of houses opens up the campus of ❿ **Alverno College,** a four-year Roman Catholic liberal arts college primarily for women. (Men are admitted as master's program students.) The college was founded in 1887 as St. Joseph's Normal School by the School Sisters of St. Francis, an international group of pretty righteous women whose "mothership" is featured in the Historic Layton walk, page 158. In 1946, Alverno took on its current name. It offers programs in business and education, a Master of Science in nursing, and an excellent arts program. In 1977, Alverno started its popular Weekend College, the first of its kind aimed at serving working women in the Milwaukee area.

Turn left on West Morgan Avenue and then left (north) on South 39th Street. Continue around the Alverno campus and take a right on West Ohio Avenue to start heading east.

Turn left (north) on South 35th Street. Note the round shape of the Zablocki branch of the Milwaukee Public Library, built in 1963.

In less than half a mile, take a left on West Kinnickinnic River Parkway, leaving busy 35th Street for a wide green zone. At West Forest Home Avenue, return to the transit stops or cross Forest Home Avenue to head back into Jackson Park.

Points of Interest

1. **Jackson Park** 3500 W. Forest Home Avenue, 414-257-7275, countyparks.com
2. **El Rey Family Market** 5200 W. Oklahoma Ave., 414-541-5200, elreyfoods.com
3. **Discount Liquor** 5031 W. Oklahoma Ave., 414-545-2175, discountliquorinc.com
4. **American Serb Hall** 5101 W. Oklahoma Ave., 414-545-6030, americanserbmemorialhall.com
5. **St. Sava Serbian Orthodox Cathedral** 3201 S. 51st St., 414-545-4080, stsava-milw.org
6. **Maria's Pizza** 5025 W. Forest Home Ave., 414-543-4606, facebook.com/mariaspizzamke
7. **Brass Key Restaurant & Lounge** 4952 W. Forest Home Ave., 414-321-7090, brasskeyrestaurant.com
8. **George Webb** 4845 W. Forest Home Ave., 414-249-4100, georgewebb.com
9. **Di Stefano's Pizza Palace** 4630 W. Forest Home Ave., 414-321-9600, distefanospizza.org
10. **Alverno College** 3400 S. 43rd St., 414-382-6000, alverno.edu

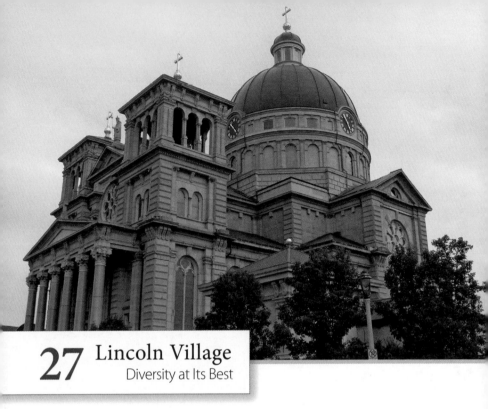

27 Lincoln Village
Diversity at Its Best

Above: The Basilica of Saint Josaphat

BOUNDARIES: W. Becher St., W. Lincoln Ave., S. Seventh St., S. 21st St.
DISTANCE: Approximately 3 miles
DIFFICULTY: Easy
PARKING: Park on Seventh St., north of Lincoln Ave.
PUBLIC TRANSIT: MCTS routes 53 (Lincoln) and 80 (Sixth St.)

As part of the Historic South Side, which originally centered on Mitchell Street, the Lincoln Village neighborhood was founded by Milwaukee's large Polish community in the late 19th century and offered more housing and another commercial area for this population. Today, it's one of the most culturally, ethnically, and economically diverse communities in the state, with many residents from Mexico, Central America, and South America. Thus, the neighborhood is rightly home to the only Salvadoran restaurant in the city, as well as other unparalleled delights.

Lincoln Village is the most densely populated neighborhood in Wisconsin—often described as having an old-world, European feel—and with houses very close together. The focal point of the neighborhood is undoubtedly the Basilica of St. Josaphat, rebuilt to its current appearance in 1901 after a fire destroyed the original structure. The dome—arguably the most beautiful in Milwaukee—and the interior were completely refurbished in the 1990s and have been in an ongoing state of restoration ever since.

The entrepreneurial spirit of both the Polish and Mexican residents has contributed to decades of commercial activity in the area. Though perhaps incongruous to some at first glance, the inter-mingling of these two similar cultures has made an enduring impact on Milwaukee's South Side.

Walk Description

Begin on North Seventh Street, north of West Lincoln Avenue, across from the 3-acre pond at ❶ **Kosciuszko Park,** home to panfish and largemouth bass. There are often geese milling about, and they can get cranky, so try to steer clear of them. The park is named after Polish general Thaddeus Kosciuszko, who fought for the victors in the American Revolutionary War, and features Kosciuszko Community Center—complete with a boxing ring inside—and Pelican Cove, one of Milwaukee County's three public water parks.

Walk north, with the park on your left. ❷ **Koz's Mini Bowl,** a Milwaukee treasure, opened in 1978 and features four duckpin bowling lanes requiring human pinsetters. Bowling leagues still compete regularly, and three generations of neighborhood teens have handled the pin setup. Koz's is as classic Milwaukee as it gets.

Take a left (west) on West Becher Street. As you walk along the north end of Kosciuszko Park, Milwaukee Public School's South Stadium is on your right. Cross West Windlake Avenue, one of those streets that cut diagonally across the grid—a much-debated feature in 19th-century street planning—making for interesting corners and variety in living and serving to move traffic quickly out of the center of the city.

❸ **St. Hyacinth** church is on the right at South 14th Street. In his neighborhood opus, John Gurda offers an interesting way of thinking about the development of the Polish South Side, which, he writes, "can be traced, in fact, by following the progress of its steeples" from the first two, both on St. Stanislaus church on Mitchell Street. St. Hyacinth's steeple rose up in 1883 as Polish immigrants and their descendants moved west.

Six blocks and 25 years later, ❹ **St. Adalbert's** steeple appears near Becher's intersection with Forest Home Avenue. Adalbert is one of Milwaukee's Polish Cathedral–style churches. This highly ornamental style of architecture is found in Catholic churches throughout the Great Lakes region.

Take a left on West Forest Home Avenue, another splendid diagonal, then another left to cut down a couple of short blocks on South 21st Street, which is lined with older frame housing and one-and-a-half-story bungalows that are sporadically present throughout the neighborhood, to West Lincoln Avenue. Forest Home Cemetery is across the street.

On the corner sits ❺ **Holler House,** which opened in 1908. This tavern has the oldest sanctioned tenpin bowling alley in the United States. The two lanes are still tended by human pinsetters, while dozens of bras hang from the ceiling in the bar. The current owner says the tradition was started by his grandmother, who encouraged women to leave a bra behind after their first visit. Many are signed by the women and other people who were in the bar at the time. Holler House is also a "cribbage bar," with a designated cribbage night once a week.

Turn left on West Lincoln Avenue. ❻ **Tsunami Restaurant** is an understated joint with limited seating, most of it at a lunch counter. They serve excellent Mexican seafood, which is what makes a seat hard to find.

In five blocks, turn right (south) on South 15th Place and then left on West Windlake Avenue. ❼ **Ss. Cyril and Methodius Parish** has served both English- and Polish-speaking families of Milwaukee since 1893. To this day it runs a Catholic Polish Saturday School, where children practice the Polish language while learning Polish culture, geography, literature, and history.

Continue on Windlake to West Lincoln Avenue and take a right. Note ❽ **Tres Hermanos Restaurant,** one of hundreds of Mexican restaurants on the South Side. This one stands out because it has a large patio and a large bar that's separate from the dining room, and it serves breakfast, lunch, and dinner. Dare we say, it's common knowledge that Mexican food is delicious for lunch or dinner (hi, tacos!), but you haven't lived until you've tried a quality huevos rancheros for breakfast.

On the south side of the street of the next block is ❾ **A & J Polish Deli.** Since 1948, this family-owned Polish deli and grocery store has sold smoked Polish sausages, hams, breads, cheeses, desserts, spirits, and many other food and drink items imported from Poland. Most of the products are labeled in both English and Polish.

Across the street, ❿ **Chet & Leona's Floral Shop,** opened in 1950, is the second-oldest flower shop in Milwaukee. (Welke's Florist on North Avenue is the oldest.) The classic shop offers fresh-cut bouquets, house and yard plants, and seasonal garden supplies. Chet & Leona's also has an online shop for 24-hour service.

A couple of blocks down on the right, ⓫ **Ben's Cycle** has been an anchor on the street since 1928. The still-family-owned business is now in the hands of the original owner's grandson. Ben's specializes in hard-to-find, high-quality bicycle products at affordable prices, and they sell

Kosciuszko Park features one of Milwaukee County's three water parks.

and service every bicycle imaginable. Since 2002, Ben's Cycle has also been the home of the Milwaukee Bicycle Co., which offers American-made, semicustom frames and accessories for single-speed bicycles.

Continue east down Lincoln Avenue for three blocks. Urban Anthropology's **12 Old Southside Settlement Museum** has history literally spread across several rooms on the ground floor of an almost 115-year-old house; each room represents different families at different time periods in the surrounding neighborhoods. The museum grew out of the studies that anthropologists in Urban Anthropology Inc. (UrbAn) have been conducting for 20 years. UrbAn claims it's the only nonprofit group of its kind "that studies people in their own backyards." The museum has limited hours, so call ahead if you plan to visit.

On the corner, **13 Rozga** funeral home has been in business for more than 120 years, operated by five generations of Rozgas. According to information from UrbAn, the Rozga family, who owned two funeral homes at the time, offered free funerals to families who could not pay during the Great Depression.

The Basilica of Saint Josaphat is now directly across the street. Being so majestic, it's worth a walk around its entire block. Take a left on South Seventh Street at the funeral home; parish offices and parking are now on the left.

Turn right on West Hayes Avenue, with the rear of the basilica to your left, and then left on South Sixth Street. The aptly named **14 El Salvador Restaurant** is across the street. This is

Milwaukee's only restaurant serving Salvadoran cuisine with classic pupusas (flatbread stuffed with meat, cheese, legumes and/or vegetables), other traditional dishes, and usually a selection of hard-to-find Central American cerveza.

Turn left on West Lincoln Avenue and get to the front of the towering ⑮ **Basilica of Saint Josaphat.** Saint Josaphat Parish was formed in 1888 and was the largest Polish parish in Wisconsin. Its first home was a smaller building that burned to the ground in 1889. The extraordinary new structure with its massive dome was modeled after St. Peter's in Rome in what was called the Polish Cathedral style of architecture. It was completed in 1901. According to Bobby Tanzilo in an *OnMilwaukee* article, the cathedral was built primarily by parishioners, many of whom mortgaged their homes to pay for the construction. There were so many leftover materials from the project that a second building was later built across Lincoln Avenue with remaining parts. Today, the basilica is one of 82 "minor" basilicas found in the United States. In 2019, a new lighting system was installed to illuminate the dome. Aside from spiritual services and events, the Basilica hosts open-to-the-public concerts by the Milwaukee Symphony Orchestra, Bel Cantos Chorus, and Concord Chamber Orchestra.

Across the street from the Basilica, Mauricio Ramirez spray-painted a new ⑯ **mural** dedicated to the frontline workers of the COVID-19 pandemic. The mural, located on the east-facing wall of the building on the corner of South Sixth Street and Lincoln Avenue, depicts what appears to be a praying health care worker along with flags of the United States and Puerto Rico. Ramirez has painted dozens of murals in Milwaukee, including a mural of the late Selena Quintanilla-Pérez in Walker's Point (Walk 12, page 66).

Catch the buses back on the corner or take a right on South Seventh Street to return to the beginning of the walk.

Points of Interest

❶ **Kosciuszko Park** 2201 S. Seventh St., 414-257-7275, countyparks.com

❷ **Koz's Mini Bowl** 2078 S. Seventh St., 414-383-0560, kozsminibowl.com

❸ **St. Hyacinth** 1414 W. Becher St., 414-645-1455, stanthony-sthyacinth.org

Lincoln Village

4. **St. Adalbert** 1923 W. Becher St., 988-0228, archmil.org/Parishes/St.AdalbertMilwaukeeF04.htm

5. **Holler House** 2042 W. Lincoln Ave., 414-647-9284

6. **Tsunami Restaurant** 2001 W. Lincoln Ave., 414-255-7759

7. **Ss. Cyril and Methodius Parish** 2515 S. 30th St., 414-383-3973, cmmk.org

8. **Tres Hermanos Restaurant** 1332 W. Lincoln Ave., 414-384-9050, treshermanosmke.com

9. **A & J Polish Deli** 1215 W. Lincoln Ave., 414-643-7733

10. **Chet & Leona's Flower Shop** 1200 W. Lincoln Ave., 414-645-0774, clflowers.com

11. **Ben's Cycle** 1013 W. Lincoln Ave., 414-384-2236, benscycle.com

12. **Old South Side Settlement Museum** 707 W. Lincoln Ave., 414-672-8090, urban-anthropology.org/Museuminfo.html

13. **Rozga Funeral & Cremation Services** 703 W. Lincoln Ave., 414-671-5200, rozgafuneral.com

14. **El Salvador Restaurant** 2316 S. Sixth St., 414-645-1768, elsalvadormke.com

15. **Basilica of Saint Josaphat** 2333 S. Sixth St., 414-645-5623, thebasilica.org

16. **Mauricio Ramirez mural** Corner of South Sixth Street and Lincoln Avenue

28 Historic Layton Boulevard
Vintage Homes and The Domes

Above: Homes on Frank Lloyd Wright's Burnham Block

BOUNDARIES: W. Evergreen Lane, W. Burnham St., S. 16th St., S. 29th St.
DISTANCE: Approximately 4.25 miles
DIFFICULTY: Easy
PARKING: S. 28th St., just north of W. Burnham St.
PUBLIC TRANSIT: MCTS route 54 (Burnham) and Purple Line (Layton)

Architect and designer Frank Lloyd Wright was a lifelong Wisconsin resident, and his structures exist throughout the state, including an entire block of homes on the east end of the Burnham Park neighborhood.

This walk spends some time on Historic Layton Boulevard, which was once Milwaukee's city limit, and circles through the Mitchell Park neighborhood and the Clarke Square neighborhood, one of Milwaukee's most densely populated. According to Urban Anthropology, the area of Mitchell Park was once a Potawatomi village and the home of Jacques Vieau, the first white settler in Milwaukee, who built a cabin there overlooking the Menomonee River in 1795. Clarke Square was established before Milwaukee became a city, basically by real estate speculators Lydia and Norman Clarke from Racine.

Perhaps the most outstanding feature on this walk is the Mitchell Park Horticultural Conservatory, referred to simply as The Domes.

Walk Description

After parking on South 28th Street, which dead-ends just north of Burnham Street, walk south to the end of the block and turn left (east) onto West Burnham Street. The houses on the left side of the street comprise ❶ **Frank Lloyd Wright's Burnham Block.** Wright, an architect, interior designer, writer, and educator born in Richland Center, Wisconsin, designed structures that he called organic architecture, meaning he incorporated the natural habitat into his designs. Wright designed these six American System-Built Homes from 1915 to 1917 while he was also working on the Imperial Hotel in Tokyo. Wright's vision was to create small, affordable housing that is believed today to have been far ahead of its time in design, philosophy, and execution. Tours run throughout the year—check the website—and if you can catch one, do so.

After that, walk to the corner and take a left (north) on Historic Layton Boulevard. The wide street includes one of Milwaukee's most beloved boulevards. In the summer and fall, it is bursting with colorful flowers planted by city workers. Walk three blocks, noticing the range of housing stock, from massive Queen Annes to modest cottages. The diversity of the homes represents the economic integration of families living in the area over the times they were built. Today, some of the homes are in need of repair or are in the process of being rehabbed by artistically minded millennials. While walking, look for carriage barns and custom-built garages that mirror the architecture of the houses.

On the left at West Orchard Street is the ❷ **School Sisters of Saint Francis.** These buildings are the Sisters' international headquarters, or mothership. Founded in 1874, the School Sisters is an international community of 1,300 women in the United States, Europe, Latin America, and India working to create a positive global impact through education and social justice. Among the ways they've done this in Milwaukee is by founding the normal school that later became Alverno College (see Walk 26, page 147) and the Layton Boulevard West Neighbors, an organization of community partners that focuses on housing rehabilitation and economic redevelopment to strengthen the neighborhoods of Silver City, Layton Park, and Burnham Park, where the Sisters' mothership is located.

Take a left (west) on busy National Avenue. The ❸ **Mitchell Park Shopping Center** was the site of a streetcar station for many decades until it was torn down in 1959 for this bit-of-an-eyesore strip mall. Today, one can thrift shop at the Value Village, one of a chain of secondhand shops, or grab a doughnut at the old-school Honeydip Donuts.

Continue west on National to North 29th Street and take a right. The houses here are just as varied as on Historic Layton. Walk north to the dead end and see the old ❹ **Falk Brewery,** which is partially obscured by trees. German immigrants Frederick Goes and Franz Falk opened the brewery in 1856 under the name Bavaria Brewery and by the late 1800s had changed the name to Falk, Jung & Borchert. It was, at one time, the fourth-largest brewery in Milwaukee, after Pabst, Schlitz, and Blatz. The brewery experienced two fires in the late 1800s and after the second fire the company was sold to Pabst in 1892.

In 2019, according to *OnMilwaukee*'s Bobby Tanzilo, members of MobCraft Brewing, a craft brewery in Madison and Milwaukee's Walker's Point neighborhood (Walk 12, page 66), collected wild yeast from the existing lagering caves on the site and made a beer, called Gier Bier, out of it.

Turn around and go back to West Pierce Street. Take a left (east). Go one block and then turn left on South 28th Street. Tucked away on this otherwise quiet residential street is the headquarters of Hatco Corporation. The employee-owned company has been in the business of developing and manufacturing food-service equipment since 1950.

Turn right on West Evergreen Lane. This street crosses Layton and leads right into ❺ **Mitchell Park Horticultural Conservatory.** The conservatory features three 85-foot-high glass domes that are filled with plant life. The Show Dome is the main dome, with seasonal themes; the Tropical Dome has more than 1,000 plants, many of which bear fruit; and the Arid (Desert) Dome displays plants from the dustier climes of the Americas and Africa. The sunny, temperature-controlled

The Domes at Mitchell Park Horticultural Conservatory

Journey House Packers Stadium, donated by the Green Bay Packers in 2013

domes are particularly coveted on very warm or extremely cold days because they provide a few-hour "vacation" for guests.

In the summer of 2019, the Mitchell Park Conservatory Task Force approved a $66 million proposal to restore the domes and upgrade Mitchell Park. The deteriorating domes will undergo restoration and expand into an urban botanical park with a restaurant, a wedding garden, an amphitheater, educational facilities, outdoor trails, and tennis courts. Head south (right, if looking at the domes), and walk on the park road to Pierce Street. Take a left on West Pierce Street.

Walk along the southern edge of Mitchell Park. Note the beautiful pond and many nature areas. In the park at South 22nd Street, take note of the football field; its fence and goalposts are set back to the left. The ❻ **Journey House Packers Stadium** officially opened on June 6, 2013. The Green Bay Packers donated the professional playing field, which was once part of the team's practice facility in Green Bay, to the Journey House.

Today, the Journey House Youth Football League and Cheerleading Program serves more than 100 low-income youth ages 6–14. During football season, seven or more games are played on this field every weekend.

Keep walking east on Pierce; the ❼ **Knitting Factory Lofts** are at the dead end of South 21st Street to the left. Named after the 1912 building's original tenant, the Van Dyke Knitting Company, this factory later served as a training facility for Goodwill Industries and is where that organization's occupational therapy programs were first developed. The building now features 100 loft-style apartments, some of which are rented at reduced rates through Wisconsin's affordable housing programs.

Continue along Pierce's old industrial corridor to ❽ **Oscar's Pub & Grill,** known for its "Big O" burger, homemade fries, and friendly owner, Oscar Castañeda, who started his career working at Sobelmans on Saint Paul Avenue. It opened in 2011 but became an instant Milwaukee classic. In 2018, a second location called Oscar's Winner's Circle opened in the Burnham Park neighborhood.

Take a right on South Cesar E. Chavez Drive (South 16th Street). Take a right (west) on West National Avenue. Walk a few blocks, passing ❾ **Phan's Garden** on the left, noting its large mural depicting temples and lush forests. Phan's is a Vietnamese and Chinese restaurant with all-pink decor and great food. Go for the bon bo bue (rice noodles with pork and beef) or one of their many bowls of delicious pho.

Adjacent to Phan's is the ❿ **Lao Buddhist Temple.** This Theravada temple is in a 1927 Spanish Colonial–style building that once housed a fraternal organization known as the Knights of Pythias, which disbanded in 1980.

Take a left on South 21st Street. Longfellow Public School is two blocks ahead on the right, with the Journey House at its southern end. Take a right on West Scott Street. The ⓫ **Journey House** is a 50-year-old organization that empowers Milwaukeeans with education, youth development, workforce readiness, and positive relationship building so they can move out of poverty.

Take a right on North 23rd Street and a left on West Vieau Place, which runs only one block alongside the southern end of ⓬ **Clarke Square Park.** According to historian John Gurda, the land was set aside for a public park in the original 1837 plans for the subdivision but was not developed until 1890.

Turn left on South 24th Street. At West Scott Street, hang a right, and walk three blocks back to South Layton Boulevard. On the corner of Scott and Layton is Ascension Lutheran Church, which houses the Southside Organizing Committee, another group dedicated to community service and positive change in Milwaukee.

Turn left (south) on Layton Boulevard, then walk back to Burnham, taking another look at the diverse mix of homes, many of which were built in the late 1800s for a new managerial class of folks who had moved out to what was once the edge of town for more space and to display their status. But, again, also note the diversity in the housing stock from the later homes that appeared throughout the 20th century.

Return to West Burnham Street. Transit stops are here, or turn right to return to the beginning of this walk.

Historic Layton Boulevard

Points of Interest

1. **Frank Lloyd Wright's Burnham Block** Burnham Street between South 28th Street and South Layton Boulevard, 414-368-0060, wrightinmilwaukee.org

2. **School Sisters of Saint Francis** 1545 S. Layton Blvd., 414-384-1515, sssf.org

3. **Mitchell Park Shopping Center** 2716 W. National Ave.

4. **Falk Brewery** (historic site) 639 S. 29th St.

5. **Mitchell Park Horticultural Conservatory** 524 S. Layton Blvd., 414-257-5600, county.milwaukee.gov/EN/Parks/Explore/The-Domes

6. **Journey House Packers Stadium** West Pierce Street at South 22nd Street, journeyhouse.org/stadium.html

7. **Knitting Factory Lofts** (private residences) 2100 W. Pierce St., 414-645-5505, knittingfactoryloft.com

8. **Oscar's Pub & Grill** 1712 W. Pierce St., 414-810-1820, oscarsonpierce.com

9. **Phan's Garden** 1923 W. National Ave., 414-382-4522

10. **Lao Buddhist Temple** 1925 W. National Ave.

11. **Journey House** 2110 W. Scott St., 414-647-0548, journeyhouse.org

12. **Clarke Square Park** 2330 W. Vieau Place, 414-257-7275, countyparks.com

29 Polonia
The Old South Side

Above: There's always a line at Leon's.

BOUNDARIES: W. Cleveland Ave., W. Holt Ave., S. 13th St., S. 27th St.
DISTANCE: Approximately 4.25 miles
DIFFICULTY: Easy
PARKING: Free street parking on Cleveland Ave. and 27th St.
PUBLIC TRANSIT: MCTS Purple Line

This walk includes parts of the Forest Home Hills, Southgate, and Morgandale neighborhoods but centers on Polonia. Although the name means "Polish community," Polonia is a neighborhood of mostly Mexican Americans. According to government data, there are also a number of families here whose country of origin is Germany, but the vast majority are US-born citizens— descendants of immigrants from Mexico and, not that long ago, parts of present-day Poland.

Polonia used to be at the southern end of what is alternatively called the Old South Side and the Historic South Side, which spanned Greenfield to Oklahoma Avenues from north to south and First to 27th Streets from east to west.

Reflecting in 2013 on how "impermanence is all that lasts," Milwaukee historian John Gurda wrote of the changing demographics of the Old South Side, noting that in 1980, 40% of this larger area's residents identified as Polish, whereas 30 years later 70% of the population is Latino (itself not a homogeneous group) and 11% identify as African American.

The numbers are a little different in the smaller segment of Polonia, but it's all adequately summarized by the business improvement district's chosen name for its 13th Street commercial strip: Crisol Corridor. On Crisol, which means "melting pot" in Spanish, there are many local retailers offering clothing—especially Western wear—along with musical equipment. There's also an Indian grocery and the city's first natural-foods store, as well as bars, auto parts stores, bodegas, jewelers, a couple of banks, a whole lot of working-class folks, and some excellent Mexican food trucks, including Taqueria Arandas, Taqueria El Cabrito, Tacos El Charrito, and J C Kings Tortas.

Walk Description

Start on the west side of South 27th Street near the intersection of West Cleveland Avenue. For many years, a man has been parked here from midsummer into autumn selling Mississippi watermelons out of his pickup truck. If he is there when you are, buy one; the watermelons are delicious.

Walk south toward ❶ **Greenwood Cemetery** on the southwest corner of the intersection. Greenwood is one of the oldest Jewish cemeteries in Milwaukee, dating to 1871, and was among the first Wisconsin cemeteries to offer land for natural, or green, burials. Maynard Steel Casting foundry is just south of that, founded in 1913 and still in operation today.

Across 27th and just to the other side of the Kinnickinnic River stands ❷ **Aurora St. Luke's Medical Center** (St. Luke's Hospital), which was founded in Walker's Point in 1928 through the acquisition of Hanover General Hospital. The current site was built in the 1950s and was the first hospital in the nation with a heart-care team on site 24/7, 365 days a year.

One block south of St. Luke's and across busy Oklahoma Avenue is ❸ **Leon's Frozen Custard,** a drive-up custard stand with house-made frozen custard that's open year-round. Founded in 1942 by a man named Leon Schneider, Leon's still claims via its sign to be the Home of the World's Finest Frozen Custard. This, however, is a point of controversy for some Milwaukeeans, who argue other custard makers—particularly Kopp's Custard—is better. However, Leon's might

South 13th Street, or Crisol Corridor, is a melting pot of stores and restaurants.

most reflect Milwaukeeans' commitment to custard because, despite the weather—including below-zero temperatures or blizzards—there are almost always customers standing outside the beloved local landmark, waiting for their turtle sundae or scoop of butter pecan.

On the other side of 27th, ❹ **Mazos Hamburgers** is a family-owned and -operated restaurant that opened its doors in 1934. When John Mazo opened this South Side diner, burgers cost 5 cents. Today, Mazo's original recipe is still used, but the price has increased to a wee bit more than a nickel. All sandwiches, including the classic-diner-delicious grilled cheese, come with sides—something Mazos offered long before other chains—of fries, soup, baked beans, cottage cheese, coleslaw, or apple sauce. The family makes all of their own soups, chili, and coleslaw dressing, and June's homemade cheese pie is a favorite among regulars.

Continue south to West Euclid Avenue. The large commercial area beyond Our Lady Queen of Peace church is the Southgate shopping area. The site of Milwaukee's first mall in 1951, it's now home to a national chain and several surrounding strip malls, a movie theater, and a drugstore. Another few storefronts south of Euclid and definitely worth a shout-out is ❺ **Ned's Pizza**, an iconic Milwaukee pizzeria with crispy, thin crust that's been around since 1969. At one time there were five Ned's locations, but today this is the sole parlor. Weekend after weekend, the small waiting area and dining area are packed. Ned's big claim to fame is that they delivered 39 pizzas to Paul McCartney and his staff when he was in town for a gig about a decade ago. The receipt is still showcased on the wall.

Turn left on West Ohio Avenue and then left on South 25th Street, across from Southlawn Park. Walk two blocks to West Oklahoma Avenue. Across Oklahoma is ❻ **Casimir Pulaski High School,** part of the Milwaukee Public Schools district. The school was named after revered Polish general Casimir Pulaski, who fought in George Washington's army during the American Revolutionary War.

Turn right on Oklahoma and walk about half a mile, past mostly bungalows and other single-level dwellings, to the ❼ **Milwaukee Fire Historical Society.** Inside a former firehouse built in 1927, this unique space became a museum in the mid-1990s and is set up like an active firehouse, with sleeping rooms, a kitchen, and a locker room. Also on display are fire-related artifacts, including vintage vehicles, such as convertible fire trucks and Milwaukee's first Cadillac ambulance; a call box; a fire-reporting telegraph system; and multitudes of photos. The museum is open to the public one Sunday a month or by appointment.

Turn right (south) on South 16th Street. In 1925 Louis Wisniewski opened ❽ **National Bakery & Deli** in what was then the mostly Polish Old South Side. Often ranked the number-one bakery in Milwaukee, on Fat Tuesday lines of customers waiting to buy pączki curl out the door and around the corner. Pączki (pronounced pawnch-key) are Polish donuts with fillings such as blueberry, buttercream, custard, lemon, prune, raspberry, and strawberry. Perhaps surprising to some, prune is one of the most popular and often the first to go when a dozen are brought into the office.

Across the street, St. Francis Hospital was founded in 1941 by the Felician Sisters. The structures across the street came about starting in the 1950s to serve Milwaukee's South Side residents.

Continue south on 16th to pass the St. Alexander parish buildings, and take a left (east) on West Holt Avenue.

Walk four blocks and then turn left on South 13th Street. The recently named Crisol Corridor area features numerous shops and restaurants, both old and new. ❾ **Bombay Sweets** is a casual, vegetarian Indian restaurant and a large bakery with Indian, Pakistani, and Bengali sweets. The menu, also substantial with more than a dozen curries, kormas, mixed platters, samosas, and more, is posted on the wall, and diners order at the counter before taking a seat in the dining area with a small-cafeteria vibe. The food is incredibly good, incredibly cheap, and served on Styrofoam plates.

In the same strip mall is Best Food Store, an Indian and Pakistani grocer open since 2001. The small space is well organized yet packed with bags of rice and other dry goods, kitchen items, produce, pastes, spices, snacks (so many bags of savory snacks!), incense, naan, oils, ready-to-eat entrées, cards with pretty adhesive bindis ready to adorn women's foreheads, and so much more. Best Foods also has a Bollywood DVD-rental section.

Across Holt to the north, Lincoln Music House is a family-owned music shop that opened in 1945. On the main floor is a good selection of new musical instruments, and on the building's lower level there is also an incredible used-accordion section. Because of the popularity of polka music in Milwaukee—thanks to the number of Polish immigrants—accordions are the unofficial instrument of the city. Lincoln also rents and repairs musical instruments of all kinds.

Turn left (north) on South 13th Street. Continue for seven blocks (about 0.9 mile) through the Crisol Corridor.

Along the way, note the small but mighty ⑩ **Natural Food Shop** that opened in 1960 and continues to serve teas, spices, herbs, supplements, homeopathics, essences, oils, organic foods, and books that support good health.

Turn left (west) on West Cleveland Avenue and walk about a quarter mile. Here is Pulaski Park, 26 acres owned by Milwaukee County with a popular hill for sledding in the wintertime along a renaturalized urban river valley.

Cross South 20th Street. Extending in both directions is ⑪ **Forest Home Cemetery.** Established in 1850, this historic cemetery with more than 110,000 burial sites includes some of Milwaukee's notable former residents, such as Jacob Best, founder of the Pabst Brewing Company; Christopher Sholes, inventor of the modern QWERTY keyboard; Frank Zeidler, Milwaukee's Socialist mayor for three terms and 1976 US presidential candidate; and William Davidson, cofounder of Harley-Davidson Motorcycles. Note Chapel Gardens, an outdoor community mausoleum drenched in extraordinary plants and flowers in the summertime, and the Gothic-style Historic Landmark Chapel, crafted in 1890.

The massive property spans 200 acres, and with thousands of trees, fountains, a small lake, and well-maintained sites, it's a peaceful place to stroll or drive through in solace. In fact, its founders created the space for the living as much as for the dead.

Once a Brady Street anchor shop, Marlene's is now a 13th Street thrift shop and job-training site.

Polonia

Points of Interest

1. **Greenwood Cemetery** 2615 W. Cleveland Ave., 414-645-1390, greenwoodjewishcemetery.org

2. **Aurora St. Luke's Medical Center** 2900 W. Oklahoma Ave., 414-649-6000, aurorahealthcare.org

3. **Leon's Frozen Custard** 3131 S. 27th St., 414-383-1784, leonsfrozencustard.us

4. **Mazos Hamburgers** 3146 S. 27th St., 414-671-2118, mazoshamburgers.com

5. **Ned's Pizza** 3246 S. 27th St., 414-645-2400, nedspizzarestaurant.com

6. **Casimir Pulaski High School** 2500 W. Oklahoma Ave., 414-902-8900, www5.milwaukee.k12.wi.us /school/pulaski

7. **Milwaukee Fire Historical Society** 1615 W. Oklahoma Ave., 414-286-5272, tinyurl.com /firemuseummke

8. **National Bakery & Deli** 3200 S. 16th St., 414-672-1620, nationalbaking.com

9. **Bombay Sweets** 3401 S. 13th St., 414-383-3553, bombaysweetsmilwaukee.com

10. **Natural Food Shop** 3048 S. 13th St., 414-383-4330, thenaturalfoodshop.com

11. **Forest Home Cemetery** 2405 W. Forest Home Ave., 414-645-2632, foresthomecemetery.com

30 Silver City
Trails and Thai Food

Above: Plastic sheep "graze" on the green rooftops of the Silver City Townhomes.

BOUNDARIES: W. Canal St., W. National Ave., S. Shea Ave., S. 37th St.
DISTANCE: Approximately 1.5 miles
DIFFICULTY: Moderate (much of the route is slightly hilly; one part descends multiple-story exterior stairs)
PARKING: Park on 37th and Pierce Sts.
PUBLIC TRANSIT: MCTS route 23 and Blue Line are on W. National Ave. on the southern leg of the walk; route 35 is on S. 35th St. in the middle of the walk.

Today, Milwaukeeans who live outside of the Silver City neighborhood know it for restaurants with delicious Thai and other Southeast Asian food, but those who reside there also enjoy the quiet streets and proximity to nature via the Hank Aaron State Trail, Three Bridges Park, and Menomonee Valley Community Park.

Silver City got its name from the spending habits of industrial workers of the 1800s and early 1900s, who put their silver dollars toward provisions and entertainment options at businesses in the heart of this former suburb on and around 35th Street and National Avenue. Like many parts of Milwaukee, it has been inhabited in waves, first by Germans, Irelanders, and Norwegians who initially came to the Walker's Point neighborhood, and then by Croats and other Central Europeans who also moved west to Silver City. Today the area continues its national and ethnic diversity with residents of Latino, Southeast Asian, African, and European heritage.

The neighborhood has seen a strong revival in recent years, including the transformation of a pedestrian tunnel through which workers walked from their homes on the bluff to the industrial work sites in the valley. Known as the Menomonee Valley Passage, the tunnel is now an artistically painted entrance to a new bridge, both of which are part of the Hank Aaron State Trail. With a renovated former tavern now housing the Urban Ecology Center, the north end of Silver City is the gateway to a Menomonee River Valley reenvisioned with an environmental focus. This rebirth has attracted a new group of millennial homeowners, many of whom purchased their first homes in the vibrant area after being priced out of trendier, more expensive neighborhoods like Bay View and Walker's Point.

Walk Description

Begin at South 37th Street across from the ❶ **Urban Ecology Center–Menomonee Valley.** With three locations in the city, the Urban Ecology Center's mission is connecting city folk to nature in many ways. In this location, its vision is to redevelop the Menomonee Valley into a strong ecological, economic, and cultural area through participation in a $26 million project, Menonomee Valley—From the Ground Up. The plan includes transforming 24 acres of wasteland into a lush outdoor learning area; a 6-mile expansion of the Hank Aaron State Trail; and improved pedestrian/bike access into the valley.

Take a right (east) on West Pierce Street. ❷ **Escuela Verde** is an alternative public charter school with an emphasis on sustainability, student-led learning, and restorative justice. Students learn through projects that often have them interacting with members of various communities in the city.

❸ **The Wisconsin Bike Fed** is the country's largest statewide bicycle organization. Historically, Milwaukee has not been a bike-friendly city, so the mission of this group is significant: "to help make Wisconsin one of the best places in the world to ride a bike."

Pierce Street begins its uphill climb under bridge girders ahead. Just past the 35th Street bridge, which you will cross later in this walk, lies a piece of land owned by the city since the

1950s. Renamed ❹ **Arlington Heights Park** in 2000, it has been a focal point of neighborhood renewal. Arlington Heights is one of 12 play areas rebuilt as part of an initiative that renovated some of the city's most deteriorated playgrounds. In 2015 the park received new fitness areas, a rain garden, climbing structures, and a new entrance from National Avenue.

Enjoy the peaceful tree-lined streets of this relatively quiet neighborhood as you continue on Pierce and take a right on South Shea Avenue. ❺ **Mamie's Bar** is a hidden gem in the Silver City neighborhood, with weekly live blues music; one of the best jukeboxes in the city; tasty, cheap cocktails and burgers; free popcorn; and various antiques as part of the decor, including a bicycle hanging from the ceiling. The proprietor, Debra Mickey, was a single mother when she opened the bar in 1981 and is still going strong. Mamie's hosts a stage during the annual Silver City InterNational Festival, held along West National Avenue in the fall.

Take a right (west) on West National Avenue. The next block begins a stretch of restaurants with tasty food options, including ❻ **Thai Barbq,** a neighborhood favorite since 2006—try the hot pot. Across the street is ❼ **Vientiane Noodle Shop,** named after the owners' original home-town, the capital city of Laos. The restaurant offers both Thai and Laotian cuisine, but it's the Laotian food that makes Vientiane special.

Take a right on 35th Street. The tops of the ❽ **Silver City Townhomes,** which you passed right before Arlington Heights Park, are visible from either side of the bridge, but walkers on the west side will have a closer view of the flock of plastic sheep on the green roofs, which are planted with three varieties of sedum. The 20 townhomes are a rent-to-own project of Layton Boulevard West Neighbors, which focuses on revitalization efforts in the Silver City, Burnham Park, and Layton Park neighborhoods. That organization was founded by the School Sisters of Saint Francis, whose home base is on the Historic Layton walk (page 158), just to the east.

Once out on the bridge, take in the broad views of the Brewers baseball stadium to the left and Potawatomi Hotel & Casino with downtown Milwaukee just beyond to the right.

Watch for the staircases on either side of the bridge leading down to the Menomonee Valley below. The 1,200-acre Menomonee Valley was once the site of prolific manufacturing because of its accessibility to railways, rivers, and Lake Michigan. Descend either public staircase, taking in the still-stellar view but also watching your step, of course.

Once on the valley floor, ❾ **Palermo's** frozen pizza factory is just to the east toward down-town. Starting in 1964 with an Italian bakery on the East Side, immigrants and company founders Jack and Zina Fallucca quickly moved into the restaurant business and, within 10 years, frozen pizza and other packaged foods. The valley facility consolidated the company's operations in one location in 2006.

View from the 35th Street bridge

Just beyond Palermo's is the massive Rexnord Gear plant, formerly Falk Corporation, whose name can still be seen on the factory smokestack rising above the valley. Its founder was Herman Falk, the son of a now relatively unknown Milwaukee brewer named Franz Falk, whose Bavaria Brewery was in the valley just across the river (see Walk 28, page 158). At one time the fourth largest in Milwaukee, Falk's brewery was in operation from 1856 to 1892. **10 Menomonee Valley Community Park** is a striking 45 acres of restored prairie and burgeoning new forest. It extends all around the stair landing, across Canal Street ahead on both sides of 35th Street, and farther west. From the staircase landing, walk the short path to West Canal Street and hang a left (southwest).

The next intersection is with **11 West Milwaukee Road,** named after the Chicago, Milwaukee, St. Paul, and Pacific Railroad, referred to mostly as just The Milwaukee Road. The railway shops and yards that stretched northwest of this point employed thousands from Silver City and the other neighborhoods surrounding the Valley, including Walker's Point (Walks 11 and 12, pages 60 and 66) and Pigsville (Walk 9, page 49). Some sources state that the shops once encompassed 160 acres of the valley floor, which was created by literally moving the Menomonee River and filling in 60 acres of wetlands. Two smokestacks are all that's left of The Milwaukee Road's shops, which closed in 1985. The railroad itself went out of business in 1986.

Continue walking along Canal Street, which also passes through Menomonee Valley Community Park; more recent industrial buildings are along the street and fill in pockets to the right, until the large paved lots of stadium parking overtake the landscape.

At the west end of the valley, the Milwaukee County Stadium was built in 1953—the home of the Braves and later the Brewers—and in 2001 the new stadium anchoring the valley opened for the Brewers. Called Miller Park, it will soon get a new corporate sponsor, and thus a renaming, but will likely remain Miller Park to many Milwaukeeans, who have a propensity for continuing to call landmarks by old names. You can get a closer look at the stadium on the Story Hill walk, page 176.

The native plantings along Canal Street are part of the continued development of the Menomonee Valley Community Park and the Hank Aaron State Trail. Today the valley focuses on aspects of environmental health and growth, primarily soil contamination and the cleanup of vacant, toxic properties—in other words, a return to something that approximates the conditions in the valley before its industrial buildup began in the 1860s.

Continue along West Canal Street. Clear signage and the brown girders of the covered Silver City Bridge beyond will indicate where to take a left at a trailhead of the **12 Hank Aaron State Trail.** The 14-mile trail is named after Milwaukee Braves/Brewers right fielder Hank "Hammering Hank" Aaron. Aaron holds many records, including the most career RBIs, and he is the only player to hit 20 or more homers in 20 consecutive seasons. The trail runs along this walk in Menomonee Valley Community Park and Three Bridges Park on both sides of the river and is featured or accessible in a number of other routes in this book, from south of Story Hill on the west end (Walk 31, page 176) to Lakeshore State Park behind the Summerfest grounds in the Third Ward on the east end (Walk 3, page 14).

Access the bridge over the Menomonee River on the trail and the **13 Menomonee Valley Passage** beyond that, which is at the western edge of Three Bridges Park. Continue under the railroad tracks; the path winds up the bluff back to West Pierce Street next to the Urban Ecology Center and the beginning of the walk.

Projects at the Urban Ecology Center include improving pedestrian/bike access to the Menomonee Valley.

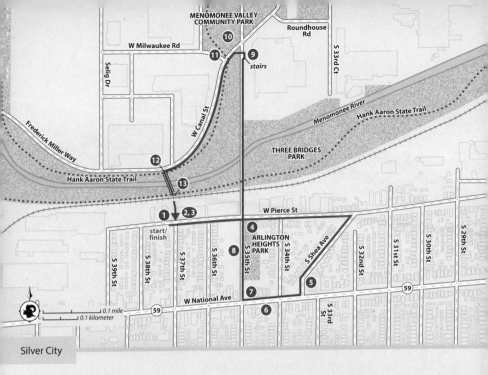

Silver City

Points of Interest

1. **Urban Ecology Center–Menomonee Valley** 3700 W. Pierce St., 414-431-2940, urbanecologycenter.org

2. **Escuela Verde** 3628 W. Pierce St., 414-988-7960, escuelaverde.org

3. **Wisconsin Bike Fed** 3618 W. Pierce St., wisconsinbikefed.org

4. **Arlington Heights Park** 3429 W. Pierce St., 414-286-8532, tinyurl.com/arlingtonheightspark

5. **Mamie's Bar** 3300 W. National Ave., 414-643-1673, mamies.net

6. **Thai Barbq** 3417 W. National Ave., 414-647-0812, thaibarbq.com

7. **Vientiane Noodle Shop** 3422 W. National Ave., 414-672-8440, vientianenoodles.com

8. **Silver City Townhomes** South 35th Street and West Pierce Street, 414-273-8326, lbwn.org

9. **Palermo's** 3301 W. Canal St., 414-643-0919, palermovillainc.com

10. **Menomonee Valley Community Park** 212 S. 36th St., thevalleymke.org

11. **Milwaukee Road** Off Canal Street just west of the South 35th Street bridge

12. **Hank Aaron State Trail** hankaaronstatetrail.org

13. **Menomonee Valley Passage** West Canal Street across from the Derse Inc. building, thevalleymke.org

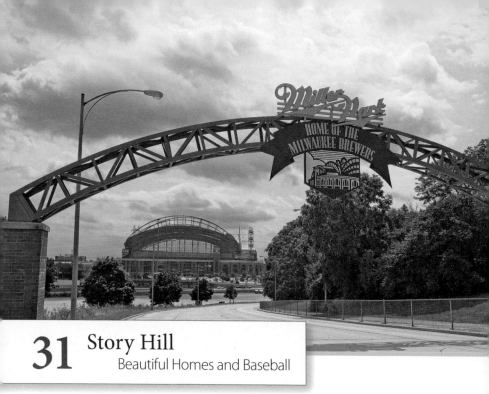

31 Story Hill
Beautiful Homes and Baseball

Above: Miller Park, home of the Milwaukee Brewers baseball team

BOUNDARIES: W. Bluemound Rd., Hank Aaron State Trail, Yount Dr., N. General Mitchell Blvd.
DISTANCE: 3 miles
DIFFICULTY: Easy
PARKING: Street parking on N. 54th St. or Bluemound Rd. (Note: There is no street parking in much of the area from an hour before to an hour after Brewers games.)
PUBLIC TRANSIT: MCTS Gold Line is on Wisconsin Ave. a block north of the walk start. Before baseball games, access the area using a Brewers shuttle from almost anywhere in the city.

The Story Hill neighborhood sits on a bluff overlooking Miller Park (to be renamed American Family Field in 2021). Thus, during the summer months, the smell of brats and burgers from tailgaters' grills wafts in the air, sometimes also carrying the muffled voices of baseball announcers into the neighborhood up the hill from the valley. The stadium was once the site of a quarry, and the houses on the bluff were built for the quarrymen, who were headed by Hiram and Horace Story—hence the name.

The mostly Craftsman-style bungalows, Tudors, and Prairie-style homes create a somewhat sprawling and affluent feel in the neighborhood. Yards are well maintained and some ornately planted; families reside in most of these attractive dwellings. The community has a history and a current standing as strong and committed, with many neighborhood-wide events held every year, including block parties and parades.

County Stadium was built in the valley below next to where the current stadium is located. In 1953 it became home for the Milwaukee Braves; the Brewers did not come to Milwaukee until 1970. The development of the stadium brought thousands of visitors and tourists to the neighborhood and further inspired the numerous bars on Bluemound Road. Today, the Brewers bar scene is one of the city's strongest entertainment options, with long-standing sports-themed establishments. The neighborhood has also experienced an uptick in other drinking and dining options in recent years.

Walk Description

Start on West Bluemound Road across from Calvary Cemetery at North 54th Street. ❶ **Calvary Cemetery** is the oldest existing Roman Catholic cemetery in Milwaukee. It is the resting place of many prominent Milwaukeeans, including Solomon Juneau, co-founder of Milwaukee and its first mayor; Frederick Miller of Miller Brewing Company; and Erhard Brielmaier, the architect who designed the stunning Basilica of Saint Josaphat on Milwaukee's South Side (Walk 27, page 152).

❷ **Dugout 54** is a massive sports bar with 32 taps and dozens of TVs for optimum game watching. It's also a spot to grab a bite or have a sit-down chicken dinner, pizza, or burgers with the fam. Like all of the bars in this area, Dugout 54 offers free shuttles to and from the stadium.

Until 2011, the building housed the iconic Milwaukee pub Derry Hegarty's—usually just called Derry's or Hegarty's. Its proprietor, Derry Hegarty, grew up in County Cork, Ireland, and moved to Milwaukee in 1965, opening the bar in 1972. He is remembered by friends as an extremely generous man who told many stories at the bar and liked to play jokes on people. Apparently, Hegarty once bought a live pig for his friend and competitor who owned another Irish bar. This is an Irish insult, and so his friend bought Hegarty a goat. But instead of getting rid of the goat, Hegarty kept it as a pet. Hegarty passed away at 76 from cancer and was interred at Calvary Cemetery, his headstone visible from the front door of his bar. According to long-time family friend and Milwaukee bar historian Dave Mikolajek, this was exactly what he wanted. "Derry used to say he wanted to be buried across the street so he could keep an eye on things," says Mikolajek. Be sure to wave hello to Derry when walking by!

Story Hill is a community-oriented neighborhood with well-maintained homes and organized events.

Next door, ❸ **J&B's Blue Ribbon Bar and Grill** is another hot spot for food and drink before and after baseball games—but it's known just as much as a place to watch Packers and Bucks games and for having a fish fry that's served not only on Fridays but on Wednesdays too. J&B's has an extensive food menu that includes Milwaukee-famous deep-fried cheese curds. According to Mikolajek, the building housed a fine dining establishment called Schlehlein's from the early 1900s to the middle 1990s. Schlehlein's had eight bowling lanes in the basement and offered live entertainment on Sunday nights, including an Elvis impersonator.

Next on this strip is ❹ **Kelly's Bleachers,** a classic Irish sports bar with a vibrant history, including a basement speakeasy. The name of the bar is a tribute to the original owner's nephew, Kelly. About half its current size when first opened in 1984, numerous expansions created an extra dining and pool room and an only-occasionally-open second floor with a rooftop deck. Kelly's is first and foremost a Brewers bar, with three shuttles that transport 50–350 people to every home game. Old Braves and Brewers memorabilia—from baseball cards to pennants—adorns the walls. Kelly's has more than a dozen beer taps and a full menu with chicken dinners, burgers, sandwiches, Reuben rolls, and "the best tater tots ever." You decide.

Take a right (south) on North General Mitchell Boulevard and follow it downhill as the street makes its way through the park sharing its name. Both are named in honor of Brigadier General William Mitchell, the grandson of Milwaukee railroad baron Alexander Mitchell. Although court-martialed for it, General Mitchell is remembered for his advocacy of air power in the US Army beginning in World War I.

The boulevard goes under the I-94 freeway to a fork in the road, with Parkway Drive to the left and the boulevard to the right. Veer right to stay on General Mitchell Boulevard to the Department of Veterans Affairs grounds, where Clement J. Zablocki VA Medical Center is located at its southern end. On this northern end is the National Soldiers Home Historic District—burial sites and clusters of buildings established immediately following the Civil War for Union soldiers to convalesce. Th

e main building, aptly called **5** **Old Main,** according to *OnMilwaukee* writer Bobby Tanzilo, has serviced many local veterans, including providing housing in the 1970s. Other buildings on the grounds include a library; barracks; Victorian homes that hosted chaplains, administrators, and surgeons; a governor's residence; a social hall with a bowling alley; and a firehouse. The historic landmark was vacant for a long time, but it has recently undergone major renovations and will soon have 80 bedroom units, community spaces, a fitness center, resource centers, offices, and more available for veterans. Even more conversion work is planned for the future to keep this piece of living history alive and continue its mission to improve the lives of vets.

Mitchell Boulevard curves to the right just after passing Old Main. On the curve, take a left for a brief jaunt on the Hank Aaron State Trail to, appropriately enough, the team home of the trail's namesake and the site of his 755th and final home run. Miller Park is visible, looming in fact, over the trees here at all times. Let it be your guide.

The trailhead is just past Paint Shop Road and follows along the row of old maintenance buildings. Leave the trail at the next intersection, Workshops Road, taking a left. At the curve after just a few feet on Workshops Road, go straight down another short, paved path to Frederick Miller Way, crossing at the painted walkway. The sidewalk ramp leads up to the plaza, which surrounds the ballpark. Take a right to walk counterclockwise around the stadium.

6 **Miller Park,** home to the Milwaukee Brewers, was completed in 2001, replacing County Stadium. The new stadium has a seating capacity of 41,900 and came with exciting amenities like the only fan-shaped convertible roof in North America. The roof can open and close in 10 minutes. In 2021, the stadium will be renamed American Family Field to reflect the naming rights deal with American Family Insurance, a Wisconsin-based business. The Brewers came to Milwaukee in 1970 and made it to one World Series in 1982 against the St. Louis Cardinals. The Brewers lost the series in the seventh game. Twice in their history, however, the Brewers won 12 games in a row—once in 1987 and again in 2018. Both times, George Webb, a 24-hour diner, gave out free burgers to honor a promise made in the 1940s by George Webb himself.

On the north side, the sidewalk plaza joins Brewers Way. Take a look at the names on the Walk of Fame and check out the statues of players and of Bud Selig, the former commissioner of Major

League Baseball and former president of the Brewers, who retired in 2015. He was inducted into the Baseball Hall of Fame in 2017.

Head due north on Yount Drive away from the stadium toward . . . another ballpark (well, a baseball diamond anyway), ❼ **Helfaer Field,** which is on the former site of County Stadium. Yount Drive is named for Robin Yount, a shortstop and center fielder for the Brewers from 1974 to 1993 who received two MVPs. He was inducted into the Baseball Hall of Fame in 1999. In June 2008, Yount, who is now a special instructor at the Brewers spring training in Maryvale, Arizona, released an all-natural lemonade drink called Robinade. A portion of the proceeds goes to charities like the Midwest Athletes Against Childhood Cancer (MACC) Fund.

Continue crossing as needed to the other side of the road to stay on the sidewalk along Yount Drive. Yount runs underneath the freeway and meanders back up the hill, underneath an arch signaling you're leaving Miller Park, then intersects North Story Parkway; take a sharp left here. Story Parkway doubles back toward the ballpark but above the route just traveled and along the bluff edge. An 8-acre county park, also named Story Parkway, overlooks the Brewers stadium and the Menomonee Valley beyond.

Turn right on North Pinecrest Street. The relative quiet of Story Hill, with its large lots and occasional backyard swimming pool, will begin to sink in the farther one gets from the bluff. Pinecrest meets North 49th Street at a triangle. Take a right and then turn left (west) on West Bluemound Road.

Back at Mitchell Boulevard Park, this time from the other direction, note the *Tree of Life* sculpture by Madison native and later Milwaukee teacher and artist Nancy Metz White, who also has similar tree sculptures in Enderis Park, along the Mount Mary walk (page 137).

Across the street, ❽ **Story Hill BKC** is a contemporary restaurant, coffee shop, and wine shop open for weekday lunch, weekend brunch, and dinner. The owners also operate Maxie's Southern Grill, which is on the Bluemound Heights walk (page 32). The food here is "inspired by the Upper Midwest with global technique." This results in dishes like crepes, shakshouka, Milwaukee beef tartare, pork spare ribs, and, of course, a Wisconsin cheese plate. They also serve beautiful desserts, including a warm cherry upside-down cake and a spot-on crème brûlée.

Head next door for an immediately different vibe. ❾ **Fat Valdy's** is a Mexican restaurant owned and operated by a family-owned company, the Fiesta Garibaldi Restaurant Group. They have four other restaurants in Milwaukee: Chicken Palace, La Michoacana, Fiesta Café, and Fiesta Garibaldi Mexican Grill. Fat Valdy's has a large menu and serves equally large portions. Continue on Bluemound Road to the beginning of the walk.

Points of Interest

1 Calvary Cemetery 5503 W. Bluemound Road

2 Dugout 54 5328 W. Bluemound Road, 414-259-1200, dugout54.com

3 J&B's Blue Ribbon 5230 W. Bluemound Road, 414-443-1844, jbblueribbon.com

4 Kelly's Bleachers 5218 W. Bluemound Road, 414-258-9837, kellysbleachers1.com

5 Old Main (Milwaukee Soldiers Home Historic District) General Mitchell Blvd., 414-939-4743, savethesoldiershome.com

6 Miller Park 1 Brewers Way, 414-902-4452, millerpark.com

7 Helfaer Field Yount Drive, 414-902-4332, www.mlb.com/brewers/ballpark/helfaer-field

8 Story Hill BKC 5100 W. Bluemound Road, 414-539-4424, storyhillbkc.com

9 Fat Valdy's 5108 W. Bluemound Road, 414-443-0287, fiesta-garibaldi.com

Appendix: Walks by Theme

Arts

Juneautown (Walk 1)
Third Ward (Walk 3)
Bronzeville (Walk 5)
Bay View North (Walk 7)
Walker's Point: Fifth Street (Walk 12)
West Historic Mitchell Street (Walk 13)
RiverWalk (Walk 20)
Silver City (Walk 30)

Beer

The Brewery Neighborhood (Walk 2)
Bay View North (Walk 7)
Walker's Point: Fifth Street (Walk 12)
Riverwest's Center Street (Walk 17)
Miller Valley (Walk 21)

Historical Interest

Juneautown (Walk 1)
The Brewery Neighborhood (Walk 2)
Upper East Side (Walk 4)
Bronzeville (Walk 5)
Bay View North (Walk 7)
Pigsville (Walk 9)
Brady Street (Walk 10)
Walker's Point: Second Street (Walk 11)
West Historic Mitchell Street (Walk 13)
Chavez (Walk 14)
The East Side (Walk 16)
Riverwest's Center Street (Walk 17)
Marquette (Walk 18)
Historic Concordia (Walk 19)
Miller Valley (Walk 21)
Lincoln Village (Walk 27)
Historic Layton Boulevard (Walk 28)
Polonia (Walk 29)
Silver City (Walk 30)
Story Hill (Walk 31)

Hot Spots

The Brewery Neighborhood (Walk 2)
Third Ward (Walk 3)
Bronzeville (Walk 5)
Bay View North (Walk 7)
Brady Street (Walk 10)
Walker's Point: Second Street (Walk 11)
Walker's Point: Fifth Street (Walk 12)
Silver City (Walk 30)

Nature

Third Ward (Walk 3)
Pigsville (Walk 9)
Brady Street (Walk 10)
Lakefront (Walk 15)
RiverWalk (Walk 20)
Vliet Street (Walk 22)
Northridge Lakes (Walk 25)
Silver City (Walk 30)

Neighborhoody

Upper East Side (Walk 4)
Bluemound Heights (Walk 6)
Bay View South (Walk 8)
Pigsville (Walk 9)
Brady Street (Walk 10)
Chavez (Walk 14)
Lakefront (Walk 15)
Riverwest's Center Street (Walk 17)
Historic Concordia (Walk 19)
Vliet Street (Walk 22)
Sherman Park (Walk 23)
Mount Mary (Walk 24)
Northridge Lakes (Walk 25)
Jackson Park (Walk 26)
Lincoln Village (Walk 27)
Historic Layton Boulevard (Walk 28)
Polonia (Walk 29)
Story Hill (Walk 31)

Continued on next page

Shopping & Entertainment

Juneautown (Walk 1)
The Brewery Neighborhood (Walk 2)
Third Ward (Walk 3)
Upper East Side (Walk 4)
Bronzeville (Walk 5)
Bay View North (Walk 7)
Brady Street (Walk 10)
Walker's Point: Second Street (Walk 11)
Walker's Point: Fifth Street (Walk 12)
The East Side (Walk 16)
Vliet Street (Walk 22)

Waterfront

Juneautown (Walk 1)
Third Ward (Walk 3)
Bay View North (Walk 7)
Bay View South (Walk 8)
Pigsville (Walk 9)
Brady Street (Walk 10)
Walker's Point: Second Street (Walk 11)
Lakefront (Walk 15)
RiverWalk (Walk 20)

The block-long Lindsay Building, constructed of Cream City Brick (see Walk 11, page 60)

Index

Note: Italicized page numbers indicate photographs. Page numbers followed by *(map)* indicate walking routes.

About the Authors

MOLLY SNYDER loves Milwaukee. A resident of Brew City for her entire adult life, Molly graduated from the University of Wisconsin–Milwaukee with a degree in English and even has a "Milwaukee" tattoo stretched across her left forearm. Today, she lives in Milwaukee's Walker's Point neighborhood with her partner, Royal Brevväxling (coauthor of this book); two sons, Kai River and Levi; and chihuahua sisters Frankie and Stevie. Molly has worked for *OnMilwaukee* (onmilwaukee.com) for almost two decades as a senior writer, editor, and manager. Her work with *OnMilwaukee* earned six Wisconsin Press Club awards. She appears weekly on WISN Channel 12 News, is a regular contributor on numerous radio stations, and cohosts the podcast *Dandelions: A Podcast for Women.*

ROYAL BREVVÄXLING is a writer, educator, and visual artist with a PhD in rhetoric and composition from the University of Wisconsin–Milwaukee. He works at two Milwaukee-based colleges, teaching communications and humanities courses, and regularly self-publishes zines documenting his travels with his partner, Molly Snyder, the coauthor of this book. Royal's visual art often focuses on constructions of class and gender, as well as portraits of chihuahuas Frankie and Stevie. His photographs have been published in *OnMilwaukee,* the *Milwaukee Journal-Sentinel,* and *Details* magazine, among others.